Crosscurrents / MODERN CRITIQUES

Harry T. Moore, *General Editor*

Modern Fiction

A Formalist Approach

William J. Handy

WITH A PREFACE BY

Harry T. Moore

SOUTHERN ILLINOIS UNIVERSITY PRESS
Carbondale and Edwardsville

FEFFER & SIMONS, INC.
London and Amsterdam

PS
379
H24

Copyright © 1971, by Southern Illinois University Press
All rights reserved
Printed in the United States of America
Designed by Andor Braun
International Standard Book Number 0–8093–0525–9
Library of Congress Catalog Card Number 71–156785

For my teachers—
Henrietta Littlefield
Gustav Mueller
Theodore Meyer Greene
John Crowe Ransom
Kester Svendsen
Victor Elconin

Contents

Preface

This is an extremely fine book on the modern novel, so fine indeed that this reader hopes it will reach a wide audience. William J. Handy is, among much else, a technical critic in a time when too many people who write about imaginative literature deal exclusively with the ideas the work under discussion represents. Certainly poems and novels can be philosophical, and of course the greatest of them very definitely express important ideas. But to isolate these, as if the work of art is merely a tract, is an error which too many teachers and critics commit today. It is a relief, then, to turn to Professor Handy's book and find that it applies to various works of fiction methods which he uses to enhance our understanding and (this is very important) our enjoyment.

Such terms as formal and formalist are scorned by some critics today, particularly those who have been taught to leave us with no more than a discussion of moral values. Again, such values are organically present in significant works, but ultimate judgments should never be based on these alone, for technique helps to trans-figure imaginative writing.

In the present book Mr. Handy, after a careful intro-duction, stressing meaning as well as technical develop-ment, presents expert and lively discussions of six im-portant works of modern fiction: James Joyce's "The Dead" (which has the force of a novel), Theodore Dreiser's Sister Carrie, William Faulkner's As I Lay Dying, Ernest Hemingway's The Old Man and the Sea,

Saul Bellow's Seize the Day, and Bernard Malamud's The Fixer. Most of these stories have been widely commented upon, but the reader of the present volume will find new insights into them as well as a mode of approach to novels and stories in general.

It might seem odd to find Dreiser in this company, since critics have so often pointed out his supposed technical deficiencies and the clumsiness of so much of his prose. But Mr. Handy makes a good case for discussing Dreiser in formal terms, and for doing so favorably.

Sherwood Anderson's tribute ("Heavy, heavy, the feet of Theodore . . .") suggests, in the course of the prose-poem, Dreiser's inevitable permanence, at least as a pioneer of realism. Yet, as Mr. Handy indicates, Dreiser has lasted, and promises to continue to do so, as more than a mere forerunner, even though we admit various technical ineptitudes. And Edmund Wilson in his essay "Is Verse a Dying Technique?" (in The Triple Thinkers, 1938), mentioned Dreiser, along with Dickens, Balzac, and Dostoevsky, who come through to us despite the fact that their writings were of a different kind from those of a Flaubert or a Joyce, "consummate artists in the sense that the great [epic] poets were"; the somewhat cruder writers have produced novels which were "the epics of societies, and lacking either the concision of the folk song or the elegance and distinction of the court," tending to "sprawl and swarm like the populations of the great cities they deal with. They talk the colloquial and practical language of the middle class, no longer schooled by the Renaissance teaching of the society it has superseded." Wilson's statement is a revealing one, placing Dreiser among titans; and Mr. Handy in his turn demonstrates how Dreiser in Sister Carrie presented the characters and situations with a natural understanding of the proper mode, including even "the author's presence" from time to time, altogether making this novel a powerful one. No reader who seriously studies this essay will ever again feel the same about Sister Carrie or, for that matter, about other works of Dreiser. Mr. Handy has here realized a critical achievement.

In quite another way, he also makes Hemingway's The Old Man and the Sea into an important story, even for those of us who have never rated it too highly. He speaks of Hemingway's earlier yearning (in Green Hills of Africa) for a fourth or fifth dimension in prose writing, and he believes that Hemingway was on the way to this in The Old Man and the Sea, with its "amazing combination of simple realism of narrative and complex symbolism of image," about which Mr. Handy presents a convincing argument. Joyce's "The Dead" has already been accepted as a classic short story (or novella, if you wish), whose strength was noted years ago by David Daiches, who followed so intensively the gradual breaking down of Gabriel Conroy's ego. Now, Mr. Handy has much to add to help our understanding and appreciation of the story. Similarly, he greatly intensifies the reader's comprehension of Faulkner's As I Lay Dying, although this novel has been dealt with often before. Bellow's Seize the Day and Malamud's The Fixer have received less attention, particularly the latter, perhaps because both of these writers are still in mid-career and difficult to see in perspective. But that doesn't prevent Mr. Handy from providing excellent expository criticism of their novels.

It is somewhat difficult to write a preface for the present volume; the writer of such introductory matter, who has helped to decide whether the book in question should be published, must display a certain amount of appreciation of it, though beyond ordinary praise I must state that William J. Handy's book has an almost unique value among recent studies of its kind. It really takes us inside these works of fiction, continually providing important insights and, above all else, suggesting to us a method of approach that is highly valuable. And, as stated earlier, Mr. Handy shows us how to enjoy these books, not just on the surface, but with an exploration of their elements that is in itself significant and, in the fullest critical sense, enjoyable for its exercise of what are, ultimately, human values, or, in the term so widely applied by today's students, relevant.

HARRY T. MOORE

Southern Illinois University
February 14, 1971

Acknowledgments

I wish to express my appreciation to the publishers for permission to use material from the following articles: "Towards a Formalist Criticism of Fiction," *Texas Studies in Literature and Language*, 3, No. 1 (Spring 1961); "A Re-Examination of Dreiser's *Sister Carrie*," *Texas Studies in Literature and Language*, 1 (Autumn 1959); "Saul Bellow and the Naturalistic Hero," *Texas Studies in Literature and Language*, 5 (Winter 1964); "A New Dimension for a Hero: Santiago of the *Old Man and the Sea*," *Six Contemporary Novels*, ed. W. O. S. Sutherland, University of Texas Press, 1962.

"Criticism of Joyce's Works: A Formalist Approach," originally published in *Proceedings of the Comparative Literature Symposium*, ed. Wolodymyr T. Zyla, II (Lubbock, Texas, 1969).

"As I Lay Dying: Faulkner's Inner Reporter," *The Kenyon Review* (Summer 1959). Permission granted by Kenyon College.

I also wish to express my gratitude to R. M. Davis for his perceptive reading of an earlier version of "The Formalist Approach to the Criticism of Fiction" and his valuable commentary, which was published in his collection, *The Novel: Modern Essays in Criticism*, Prentice-Hall, 1969.

Modern Fiction
A Formalist Approach

1

The Formalist Approach to the Criticism of Fiction

In the 1940s the fear of the professor of literature was that the "close attention to the text" method of the New Critics meant the abandonment of a literary scholarship with its characteristic objectivity in favor of a literary criticism that would be based necessarily on a highly subjective and largely intuitive response. Again, in retrospect, one can understand his concern. Perhaps the proponents of the new method recognized the need for objectivity when they set about creating a new critical vocabulary. Beginning with the publication of Cleanth Brooks's and Robert Penn Warren's *Understanding Poetry* in 1938, virtually every critical anthology has offered its "Glossary of Critical Terms" in an appendix, beginning with "ambiguity" and "ambivalence," and has included specialized definitions of critical terms designed to fit specialized theories of literature: terms like "tension," "paradox," "poetic belief," "poetic intention," and the like. And it was these two characteristics—"close reading of the text" and a special set of critical terms—which, more than their underlying theories, characterized and for most labeled "the new criticism." Today we speak of "formalist criticism" and our intention, I think, is to escape the narrowness of these labels and to emphasize a more significant characteristic: not "form" merely but *meaning through form*.

1

Today there is a new and seemingly counterimpulse evident in literary study: the concern of the student that what he studies be relevant to his life. The impulse, of course, is not peculiar to literary study; it apparently reaches into every aspect of young men's and women's lives everywhere. Nevertheless, its impact on the way literature is being taught in the universities has already been felt. The teacher of literature feels that he is being urged to abandon his preoccupations with literary form and attend to that content which the student feels to be "relevant." But today's teacher of literature has been influenced by the principles of the formalists, and he knows that the new demand for relevance need not be discouraged if it can be given some direction; that it need not imply a separation of content and form. For he grants that the impulse to significance is healthy enough and does not contradict the convictions of the man of letters, who is also deeply committed to a belief in significance. He would press the new student to hold to his own convictions while considering a vital modification, namely that meaning in literature is not only stated differently from meaning in the sciences or even in the various intellectual disciplines which comprise the humanities, but that the kind of meaning which is achieved through literary forms says something about human living in all its contradictory, paradoxical, and virtually inexplicable nature that cannot be retained in a conceptualized account. Here, he would say, is his faith in the relevance of literature and in the relevance of literary study.

Today's critic recognizes that the "close reading" of poems was indeed worthwhile, and he is looking for ways in which the method can be applied to the study of fiction. He is also saying, I think, that in "the close reading of fiction" we need not come to the work with a large acquisition of critical concepts that are to be applied categorically. And he is also saying that it is precisely by "the close reading of fiction" that we will get to the relevance demanded by today's students—not, of course, by offering moral abstractions, but by revealing those realizations of what it means to be a human being that are offered in and through the varied and complex literary forms that comprise the language of fiction.

Of all theorists in the formalist tradition, the one who best understood the distinctive nature of the poem's structure was John Crowe Ransom. His book *The New Criticism* (1941) was essentially a critique of the specific concepts of the poem's structure that were held by T. S. Eliot, Yvor Winters, I. A. Richards, and William Empson, whose theories had much in common with each other and with his own. After stressing the similarities and offering "corrective advices" where he felt a concept to be misguided, Ransom proclaimed that the views held by these critics of the poem, its structure, and its criticism constituted a "new criticism." His book was climaxed by a chapter entitled "Wanted: An Ontological Critic." What Ransom "wanted" was not merely a critic who recognized that poetic formulations were generically different from scientific formulations, but one who built his critical practice upon the ramifications of that ontological distinction. In short, Ransom wanted a critic whose understanding of the structure of the poem was based on ontological rather than descriptive distinctions. That is, to say with Cleanth Brooks that the structure of the poem is "organic" or "a pattern of resolutions and balances and harmonizations" was not to speak "ontologically" but descriptively.

For Ransom the structure of the poem consisted of two generally different kinds of symbolic formulations: a cognitive element which he called the poem's "logical core," and a noncognitive element which he called the poem's "texture." The distinction is a vital one in modern criticism. Indeed, it is now evident that it is this distinction that gives us the differentia of formalist criticism. We discern its presence in the most basic utterances of the century's outstanding formalists: in Pound's definition of an image as an "intellectual and emotional complex," in Eliot's concept in describing Chapman's poetry as "direct sensuous apprehension of thought," in Tate's explanation of the poem's structure in terms of "tension" and "extension." We see it implicit in Burke's concept of "symbolic action" and in Blackmur's concept of *Language as Gesture.* The same ontological distinction is present explicitly in the titles of works by later formalists: in Rahv's *Image and Idea,* Read's *Icon and Idea,* and Wimsatt's *The Verbal Icon.*

Ransom's approach to the poem followed from his concept of the poem's structure. Following the full experience of the poem as given in its individual form of presentation, the initial act of criticism he saw as cognitive: the necessity to arrive, implicitly or explicitly, at a formulation of the "logical core" of the total presentation. In his elaboration Ransom referred to the "logical core" as the "argument" and again as the "paraphrase" of the poem. He pointed out that while the critic worked primarily with the "texture" of the poem, i.e., with those devices of concretion that distinguish poetry from prose, yet the critic must also perform an accurate analytical judgment of what the poem is about; he must, in short, provide a cognitive statement of what the poem says, however inadequate any statement would be as a representation of the total poem. Ransom has stated the source of his literary theory on many occasions as grounded in Kant's aesthetics; and Kant was quite clear on the necessity of the logical faculty in aesthetic judgments. Kant wrote: "in a judgment of taste [i.e., "the faculty of judging the beautiful"], a reference to the Understanding is always involved."[1] And again in another place:

> But nothing can be universally communicated except cognition and representation [i.e., the artistic presentation] so far as it belongs to cognition. For it is only thus that this latter [the artistic presentation] can be objective; and only through this has it a universal point of reference, with which the representative power of everyone is compelled to harmonise.[2]

My point is simply to establish the necessity of recognizing the presence of the "logical core," both as a structural element in the literary presentation and as a necessary step in the critical process. T. M. Greene, who has applied Kantian principles to his examination of the major arts in his authoritative book, *The Arts and the Art of Criticism* (1940), provides a similar statement, which is helpful in understanding this vital principle concerning the "ontological" structure of a literary work:

> every word (except proper nouns and demonstratives) has a core of conceptual meaning, i.e., a symbolic reference to some distinguishable recurrent quality, relation, or pattern, and furthermore, this conceptual meaning functions even when words are used for the construction (by the writer) and the reconstruction (by the reader) of images.[3]

Ransom was not fashioning some sort of arbitrary structure for the poem when he made his distinction between its logical and nonlogical elements. What he discerned is basic to the poem as a symbolic formulation. For verification he turned first to Hegel, later to Kant. In one of his more famous essays, "Criticism as Pure Speculation," he declared:

He [Hegel] seems to make the handsomest concessions to realism by offering to knowledge a kind of universal which was not restricted to the usual abstracted aspects of the material, but included all aspects, and was a concrete universal. The concreteness in Hegel's handling was not honestly, or at any rate not fairly, defined. It was always represented as being in process of pointing up and helping out the universality. He could look at a work of art and report all its substance as almost assimilated to a ruling "idea." But at least Hegel seemed to distinguish what looked like two ultimate sorts of substance there, and stated the central esthetic problem as the problem of relating them.[4]

Here is what Ransom meant by "ontological criticism": the recognition that in the symbols of art there are "two ultimate sorts of substance" and that "the central esthetic problem" is "the problem of relating them." That is, every work of art, in whatever medium, characteristically possesses a universal aspect, which makes possible a concept of the work, and a particular aspect, which offers a presentation of meaning far in excess of what its concept is able to render.

In another of his key essays, "Poetry: A Note in Ontology," Ransom made a distinction similar to the one of the Hegel passage, this time relating his theory to Kant's aesthetics. His immediate concern was for the fundamental kinds of subject matter a poem may emphasize: "things" and "ideas." His point was the basic difference in the being of the symbols representing things and the being of the symbols representing ideas. His opening paragraph stated:

A poetry may be distinguished from a poetry by virtue of subject-matter [i.e., things and ideas] and subject-matter may be differentiated with respect to its ontology, or the reality of its being. An excellent variety of critical doctrine arises recently out of this differentiation, and thus perhaps criticism leans upon ontological analysis as it was meant to do by Kant.[5]

Kant called for a distinction to be made between the "Understanding," the faculty that reduces its object to a concept in order to classify it, and the "Imagination," the faculty that maintains its object in a presentation in order to know it as it is—undistorted by logical reduction. Kant insisted that the kinds of being represented by the two forms of the judgment were ontologically distinct.

It is now clear that Ransom's quest for a criticism that would be "ontological" expressed the direction criticism was to follow after mid-century. His "ontological" critic was to be one who would approach the work with an awareness of its fundamental structure as a distinctly *aesthetic* judgment—one which exceeds the capacity of a logical judgment by offering a concrete presentation of the texture of experience.

Ransom's critical practice was based upon his theory of the ontological structure of the poem. The steps in the process of relating his theory to his practice may be summarized as follows:

1. Every poem has a paraphrasable content, the argument or plot of the poem.

2. The important considerations for criticism are located not in the paraphrase but in the "texture" of the poems.

3. The texture is composed of devices or forms through which a concrete presentation of meaning is achieved. Some of the more common devices of concretion which have received special emphasis by various schools of modern criticism include: the symbol, the image, paradox, irony, ambiguity, myth, tone, and the like.

4. Critical procedure means the close analysis of

these formal devices, because it is in the special use of language, in the *form* it receives, that literary art becomes a unique kind of knowledge.

5. Close analysis presupposes, first, the sensibility to "re-create" (T. M. Greene's term for the initial critical act) the work, i.e., to experience it as a presentation; second, the humility to allow the work to speak its own meanings through its own form without imposing critical preconceptions upon it; and third, the full realization that the critical task is forever one of discovery.

The point I wish to emphasize in summary is that the distinctive critical practice of the early formalists had its source directly in the nature of the poetic formulation itself—in short, in the kind of structure that the poem represents.

When we consider the structure of the lyric poem and the structure of fiction in their most fundamental sense, what Ransom would call their "ontological structures," the movement from the poem to the story is not different in kind. The lyric poem, like the painting or the sculpture, expresses man's capacity to formulate his world in concrete presentations which render the full unabstracted bodiness or texture of the experience. Works of fiction accomplish all this but add a new dimension: they express man's capacity to experience his experience, not in moments merely (as reflected in the lyric poem or the painting or the sculpture), but in time.

On the surface, works of fiction appear quite different from lyric poems. Fiction is concerned with a particular world and particular characters, presented through a succession of scenes or episodes which are constructed to develop a central action. Yet the essential structure of fiction—again, what Ransom would call its "ontological" structure—is, I believe, basically the same as that of poetry.

When we consider the ontological structure of fiction, i.e., its structure as a concrete presentation, rather than as an abstract conceptual one, it is immediately apparent that the most basic unit of presentation is the scene or episode. I mean to indicate by the use of the term *episode* that unit of dramatic expressive meaning composed of one or more scenes which may be formulated by an event, or situation, or action, or a relationship between characters or an objectification of a character's state of mind, which is integral to the work as a whole, but which is distinguishable as a separate unit of presentational meaning. Sometimes the episode is given a formal designation, as in the eighteen episodes of Joyce's *Ulysses* or in the sixty-six viewpoint sections of Faulkner's *As I Lay Dying*. But often the episodes are not marked off, as in the five discernible sections of Hemingway's *The Old Man and the Sea*. But the presentational unit which more than any other distinguishes fiction from poetry is its formulation of experience as a succession of scenes or episodes. My point is that these presentational units in fiction may be viewed as being analogous to the image in poetry. That is, from an ontological point of view—that point of view which I wish to establish as the common ground for the structure of both poetry *and* fiction—both the image (the basic unit of presentation in the poem) on the one hand and the scene and episode (the corresponding presentational units of the story) on the other all possess the same generic characteristics:

1. *In both poetry and fiction meaning is presentational and nondiscursive.* (Although often seemingly discursive passages occur in fiction—i.e., chiefly author commentary and explanation. However, I believe even author commentary becomes presentational when it

takes place in the fictional form. Consider the concrete effect of Dreiser's prosaic commentary; for example, his familiar asides to his reader. My point is that Dreiser's "asides" become part of his characteristic style, his concrete form in one's overall experience of a Dreiser novel. A full discussion is given in chapter 3, "Dreiser's *Sister Carrie.*")

2. *Both forms of presentational units* (the image of the poem the scene and episode of the story) *comprise a single configuration of multiple meaning.* (Hence the variety of critical generalizations about the meaning of a work that are possible. I do not mean contradictory generalizations; rather I refer to the variety of critical insights possible *in any* concrete presentation—whether in art *or* life.)

To regard contradictory readings of a work as differing interpretations is, I believe, to confuse the creative function of the artist with the re-creative function of the critic. The difference is not merely semantic but touches on that complex problem in literary aesthetics of *the objectivity of the work.* As readers of literary criticism we do not value a critic's response to a work unless we have faith in the quality and relative objectivity of his critical judgments. We feel, I think, that the work must not be seen as some kind of Rorschach test, designed to reveal the critic's (or reader's) private response. Rather it is itself an interpretation, that distinct form of judgment concerning man's existence which Kant called the "aesthetic judgment."

We do not when we read criticism expect an interpretation of the artist's interpretation. One "interpretation" is, or should be, enough. Rather we expect the critic to be a good reader, perhaps something of an expert reader, of a special *form* of language, itself designed to give something more than language ordinarily can render. And we expect him to articulate his reading of that singular interpretation that is the artist's. In short the critic's job is more accurately described as the discovery of meaning than as the interpretation of meaning.

3. *Both forms (poetry and fiction) intend to formulate the particularity, the "texture" of experience.* (That is, as opposed to the intention in the strictly rational forms of the various intellectual disciplines, those systematic studies in the sciences and humanities, which intend to offer determining principles and classifications of man's experience. As the aesthetician T. M. Greene put it: "Art and science focus upon different aspects of reality and human experience, and the farther they advance, the more pronounced the difference between them becomes." [6] The novelist whose focus is on man in his experiencing of his world in time, whether inner or outer, and the poet whose focus is on man's non-temporal experience both possess the same characteristic concrete vision. Both see the world's concrete constitution, and both wish to celebrate precisely that aspect of its nature.)

4. *Both forms are directly primarily to sense perception, not to abstract intellection.* (Hence presentational forms like the poem and the story offer their own forms of images which are primarily to be experienced rather than conceptualized. Thus prose in fiction is so specialized a form of prose that it should not be referred to as prose. Like the poem, the story is more nearly language "dislocated into meaning," its words not words but presentations. For like the poem the language of fiction is more accurately described as the construction of devices of concretion than predications about a subject.)

5. *And finally, both forms of presentational units exceed the concept in containing more meaning than is possible of formulation in a concept.* (Hence the special

"relevance" of literature as being capable of communicating a kind of knowledge about man's experience that cannot be formulated by the sciences. As Ransom insisted: "But I may contemplate also, under another form entirely, the form of art. . . . The features which the object discloses then are not those which have their meaning for a science, for a set of practical values. They are those which render the body of the object and constitute a knowledge so radical that the scientist as a scientist can scarcely understand it. . . . The knowledge attained there, and recorded, is a new kind of knowledge, the world in which it is set is a new world.") [7]

The fictional forms (scene, episode), then, no less than the poetic image, represent the literary artist's attempt at, in Eliot's words, "transmuting ideas into sensations." When Stephen Spender wrote the following passage in his fine essay on poetic creation, "The Making of a Poem," he had, primarily, ontological considerations in mind. And the striking fact is that if we substitute "fiction" for "poetry" in the first line and "scenes" for "images" in the second, the truth of the passage is as evident as in its original sense. My point is of course the analogous, even homologous, role played by "images" in the poem and "scenes" in the novel. Mr. Spender writes:

> That is the terrifying challenge of poetry. Can I think out the logic of images? How easy it is to explain here the poem that I would have liked to write! How difficult it would be to write it. For writing it would imply living my way through the imaged experience of all these ideas, which here are mere abstractions.[8]

The passage is, of course, a remarkable statement of the formalist's most fundamental convictions. Rewritten, it provides, I believe, "a note on ontology" for fiction.

> That is the terrifying challenge of *fiction*. Can I think out the logic of *scenes and episodes?* How easy it is to explain here the *story* that I would have liked to write! How difficult it would be to write it. For writing it would imply living my way through the imaged experience of all these ideas, which here are mere abstractions.

Spender's observations recall T. S. Eliot's simple statement of the same Coleridgian insight: "There is a logic of the imagination as well as a logic of concepts." The suggestion I wish to make is that both from a creative and re-creative (critical) standpoint, fiction possesses the same ontological structure as poetry. The writer must "think out the logic" of his scenes and episodes with a logic which springs from his image-making faculty. The reader, confronted with a symbolic pattern similar to his daily experience (a progression of individual scenes), responds to the pattern with the expectancy that it will be fully as comprehensible as his daily experience. Actually he anticipates much more. The succession of scenes which are given form in a fictional work constitute a much more meaningful pattern than one's experience, because they constitute not merely a representation of experience but a *judgment about* experience.

T. S. Eliot's concept of the "objective correlative," although most often applied to the understanding of the way expressive meaning is formulated in poetry is, I believe, fully as applicable to the understanding of the way expressive meaning is formulated in drama and fiction. Indeed, Eliot conceived the principle while examining a work of drama. I believe that Eliot's "objective correlative" principle applies with equal validity to all forms of literary art. Eliot wrote:

> The only way of expressing emotion in the form of art is by finding an "objective correlative," in other words, a set of objects, a situation, a chain of events which shall be the formula of the particular emotion; such that when the external facts, which must terminate in sensory experience are given, the emotion is immediately evoked.[9]

In his poems Eliot's use of objective correlatives to express meaning with a presentational immediacy is present in nearly every line, especially in the early poems, i.e., those written prior to "Ash Wednesday" and the *Four Quartets*. Examples of objective correlatives vary from such simple images as "I have measured out my life with coffee spoons," which objectifies Prufrock's regret at the realization that he has wasted his life in the trivial values of the drawing room, to the more complex image of Prufrock himself, aware, yet trapped in a meaningless existence by the very timidity of purpose that constitutes his cultural heritage.

In fiction the form that the selected or discovered "set of objects," "situation," or "chain of events" must be presented in is the *scene* and *episode*. The lyric poem imposes no such demand, but the poem is not, as is fiction, concerned with life in action; characteristically the lyric poem is a still life; the work of fiction is life in motion, life experienced not merely in space but in time. This is not to deny Joseph Frank's excellent distinction of "spatial form in modern fiction." My intention here is simply to suggest the significance of time as one differentia of fiction whether "reflexive" as in *The Sound and the Fury* or linear as in *Sister Carrie*.

Pound was closer to a structural definition of the basic literary unit when he described the image as "that which presents an intellectual and emotional complex in an instant of time." [10] It should be noted that not only does Pound's definition suggest Ransom's distinction between the poem's logical and nonlogical elements, but Pound's term "presents" emphasizes a further characteristic, one that is equally vital in distinguishing the basic unit of literary formulation, namely the *presentational* character of the image. Further Pound considered the entire poem to be itself a single image. Again the application to the work of fiction is, I believe, appropriate. That is, the narrative images, scenes, and episodes which comprise the ontological structure of the fictional work may be seen to function reflexively in the process of their re-creation by the reader, providing finally a single overall presentation which is the work.

That the novel or story is better seen as a single image than as a linear progression can be shown in two distinct ways. First, the thematic meaning presented in the opening scene or episode of *Sister Carrie* or *As I Lay Dying* can be comprehended only in the light of the totality of scenes and episodes which constitute the work. Second, although the structure of the novel may indeed be a time structure in which a succession of related episodes define the way a work is constructed, the critic will seldom wish to follow such a pattern in the structure of his critical essay. Rather his "job of work" as a critic must be to offer generalizations not about what is happening in the various presentations as they unfold but generalizations about the themes embodied in the presentations and their relationship to each other without regard to their position in the linear progression of the work.

Throughout, my chief concern in discussing narrative forms is their presentational character, a much more complex matter, I believe, than discussing the presen-

tational character of poetic forms. The presentations
of poetry are more readily discernible. The poetic line
is compact, intentionally economic, and immediate in
its presentation of tone and image. As such it seldom
resembles the straightforward language patterns of
logical prose, and when it does, as in "After great pain a
formal feeling comes," it does so with the intentional
exploitation of the precise quality possessed by a flat
assertion, i.e., with the concrete quality gained by a
simple direct statement. In its context in the poem it is,
of course, not discursive prose, but an intentional imitation of discursive prose. We see that what the line
formulates is not so much an idea concerning great pain,
but the *presentation* of qualitative experience—here
something of the desperate assertion of a voice, the voice
of the speaker in the poem. Further, of course, it is a
metered line, one which is followed by a succession of
concrete images: "The nerves sit ceremonious like
tombs/The stiff heart questions."

On the other hand the language line of fiction, precisely because it resembles compositional prose, is much
more deceptive, much more subtle in offering its presentations. But to insist that it does offer presentational
meaning and not ideational meaning is to distinguish
the forms of fiction from those of the various intellectual
disciplines just as emphatically as John Crowe Ransom
and his followers distinguished poetry from science.

For the man of letters, whether a critic or lay reader,
the alternative to this conviction is disastrous to fiction
as an art form: the novel becomes just one more vehicle
for philosophy, or today, sociology and political science.
And what is perhaps worse, the work's meanings become
lost in the distortions that are inevitable when the focus
in reading a work of fiction is not specifically on *meaning
through its presentational forms.*

Viewed in Pound's ontological sense, the scene and
episode perform the same function for fiction that the

image performs for the poem. Consider the treatment of scene in any of Hemingway's novels or short stories. In his sharply delineated scenes, in his careful fashioning of every line to get the most out of every presentational unit, in his insistence that writing is a process of "getting it right," Hemingway constructs prose poems. His concern is always with the expressionistic qualities which are generated in literary art. One cannot help but draw the parallel to the same concern for expressionism in literature that defines the writing of another of Pound's pupils, T. S. Eliot. For both, the presentational unit must itself do the work, and with that sense of immediacy of meaning that Pound continually insisted upon.

In "The Short Happy Life of Francis Macomber" the opening scene is characteristic of Hemingway's technique, in which, following Pound's teachings, meaning is *presentational* and *immediate*:

It was now lunch time and they were all sitting under the double green fly of the dining tent pretending that nothing had happened.

"Will you have lime juice or lemon squash?" Macomber asked.

"I'll have a gimlet," Robert Wilson told him.

"I'll have a gimlet too. I need something," Macomber's wife said.

"I suppose it's the thing to do," Macomber agreed. "Tell him to make three gimlets."

The mess boy had started them already, lifting the bottles out of the canvas cooling bags that sweated wet in the wind that blew through the trees that shaded the tents.

"What had I ought to give them?" Macomber asked.

"A quid would be plenty," Wilson told him. "You don't want to spoil them."

"Will the headsman distribute it?"
"Absolutely."

If we were to mark off the scenes in the story by drawing a line between them, the first line would be drawn here.

Much of the impact of Hemingway's writing depends on the sharp demarcation between scenes. For example, the tone shift which accompanies the next scene captures the full sense of the contrast one experiences when the immediacy of a present experience is broken by a sudden shift to a past experience presented as exposition. Hemingway's second scene begins:

> Francis Macomber had, half an hour before, been carried to his tent from the edge of the camp in triumph on the arms and shoulders of the cook, the personal boys, the skinner and the porters. The gun-bearers had taken no part in the demonstration. When the native boys put him down at the door of his tent, he had shaken all their hands, received their congratulations, and then gone into the tent and sat on the bed until his wife came in. She did not speak to him when she came in and he left the tent at once to wash his face and hands in the portable wash basin outside and go over to the dining tent to sit in a comfortable canvas chair in the breeze and the shade.

It is clear that this scene, which is primarily expository, is much less concrete, hence much less vividly presentational than the dramatic opening scene. Yet the difference, I believe, is one of degree, not kind. The "exposition" is hardly that of expository writing; on the contrary the scene is dramatic in its essential function, however more recognizably cognitive than the opening scene. It is the qualitative *experience* of the cognition that is central, not the mere understanding of what is happening. And while it is unquestionably true that fiction does not offer its succession of scenes with the same degree of objective presentation that occurs in the drama, yet it is clear that the apparently discursive passages, such as description, narrative summary, and even author commentary, take on a presentational character when they are woven into the context of a scene. Within the frame of the individual scene each language unit functions expressively, or in Susanne Langer's term "non-discursively," to present an aspect of the total work—a thematic meaning, an attitude, a relationship—that is essential to the total meaning of the work. For example, in the opening scene Hemingway presents not only the world of the action and the characters involved, but he also suggests the tension of the situation, the relationship between the characters, and the all-important fact that the subject matter is to concern not so much action and event as it is individual human values. Close analysis of fiction must, I think, require a conscious awareness of these building segments that contribute to the work's presentational immediacy and dramatic structure. They are, I believe, analogous to the concrete formal structure of the poem, i.e., those devices of concretion, chiefly metaphoric, which comprise the poem's presentational meanings.

When we consider the formal difference between fiction and poetry, it is evident that one basic difference lies in fiction's concern with the presentation of character. The novelist may employ a variety of techniques for character presentation, from placing his reader within the viewpoint character by the use of the first or third person convention to dramatically objectifying the state of mind of a character by using the technique of the interior monologue. Hemingway is perhaps a good example of the first; Faulkner of the second. It would be helpful to examine a passage from a work of each writer in order to illustrate fiction's concrete presentation of the inner man.

The opening scene in *A Farewell to Arms* is typical of Hemingway's general technique and intention: to focus not so much on action and event but on the individual values of the protagonist. Thus the opening "episode" formulates in its primary function the sensibility of the hero. Further, the scene is characteristic of Hemingway's technique, in which, following Pound's teachings, meaning is presentational and immediate.

> In the late summer of that year we lived in a house in a village that looked across the river and the plain to the mountains. In the bed of the river there were pebbles and boulders, dry and white in the sun, and the water was clear and swiftly moving and blue in the channels. Troops went by the house and down the road and the dust they raised powdered the leaves of the trees. The trunks of the trees too were dusty and the leaves fell early that year and we saw the troops marching along the road and the dust rising and leaves, stirred by the breeze, falling and the soldiers marching and afterward the road bare and white except for the leaves.

The "we" viewpoint continues for the remainder of the brief two-page chapter and begins again in the opening of the second but then is abruptly dropped and the "we" becomes "I." Thus in the opening scene there are objectified those values which the viewpoint character, Frederick Henry, shares in common with his colleagues in the Italian army. Then, beginning with the change to the "I" viewpoint in the opening scene of the second chapter, the individual character is isolated, and we see the world as he sees it with *his* individual values and sensibility:

> The next year there were many victories. The mountain that was beyond the valley and the hillside

where the chestnut forest grew was captured and there were victories beyond the plain on the plateau to the south and we crossed the river in August and lived in a house in Gorizia that had a fountain and many thick shady trees in a walled garden and wisteria vine purple on the side of the house. Now the fighting was in the next mountains beyond and was not a mile away. The town was very nice and our house was very fine. The river ran behind us and the town had been captured very handsomely but the mountains beyond it could not be taken and I was very glad the Austrians seemed to want to come back to the town sometime, if the war should end, because they did not bombard it to destroy it but only a little in a military way. People lived on in it and there were hospitals and cafes and the artillery up side streets and two bawdy houses, one for troops and one for officers, and with the end of the summer, the cool nights, the fighting in the mountains beyond the town, the shell-marked iron of the railway bridge, the smashed tunnel by the river where the fighting had been, the trees around the square and the long avenue of trees that led to the square; these with there being girls in the town, the king passing in his motor car.

Again we see that the language units function in quite the same way that T. S. Eliot's objective correlatives do, namely, to present thematic meanings that contribute to the overall presentations. For example, in the opening scenes quoted Hemingway presents not only the world of the action and the central character's state of mind; he also suggests what the central conflict is to be: namely, the quest for meaning in a world which everywhere appears to be devoid of meaning. Further, the opening passages also suggest the nature of Hemingway's subject matter—one that, although highly dramatic, nevertheless is to be concerned not so much with dramatic action as with the characteristic value responses of his characters.

When we examine the passage closely we are aware that the viewpoint character has quite definite attitudes toward the world of his existence—a world of chance happenings and disappearing traditional values, a world which shows no concern for the individual, one in which he is simply an object among objects. It is, in short, a naturalistic world in which the individual will ultimately be the victim of forces over which he has no control. Yet this is not Hemingway's central subject matter, as it would be Dreiser's. Hemingway's focus is not on *what happens* to his character as he confronts a hostile, or at best indifferent, environment. Rather his focus is on the way his character *responds* to his environment. Or, said in another way, Hemingway's real subject matter is man's *way* of living his life—a subject matter which focuses first on the individual's values and sensibilities. The central character presented in the opening scenes reveals a detached, unsentimental attitude toward his world. Paradoxically, he reveals an openness to the sights and sounds of his experience, which indicates a zest, even a love of living; yet at the same time he reveals an indifference bordering on despair to what is happening in his present experience. We see that when Frederick Henry is presented as one who sees all things as possessing coordinate values—i.e., the woods, the mountains, soldiers marching and fighting—all juxtaposed with other disparate images—the girls in the town, the shady trees, the bawdy houses—the meaning which is formulated is quite complex. On one level what is suggested is the chaos of war, on another the sensibility of a young man who is open and reflective but caught at the same time in a despair, yet one which he has disciplined himself to endure. And further, we see that his despair is not merely characteristic of a private subjectivity or neurotic affliction; rather we see that the condition of his existence is sufficient objective reason for his despair. Thus, read closely, Hemingway has not offered merely exposition and description: he has engaged the thematic conflict of the work.

From an ontological point of view, a scene is a way of giving form to the way we actually encounter experience in the process of daily living. In some way each successive experience, however inconsequential, is an encounter, a confrontation, with an expressive presentation. In *Adonis and the Alphabet*, Aldous Huxley wrote:

> Whether we like it or not, we are amphibians, living simultaneously in the world of experience and the world of notions, in the world of direct apprehension of Nature, God and ourselves, and the world of abstract, verbalized knowledge about these primary facts. Our business as human beings is to make the best of both these worlds.[11]

It is the sciences which not only provide us with the "notions" and the "knowledge" but at the same time testify as one kind of symbolic form to man's impulse to abstraction. It is the arts, on the other hand, which remind us that one portion of our living experience is "the world of direct apprehension of Nature." They also testify to a knowledge impulse—the desire to give symbolic form to concrete, individual experience.

Perhaps in the bombardment of our sensibilities by the shapes and colors and sounds of ever-changing experience, we attend but little to individual presentations. That is, we make little effort to "understand" them. Perhaps we unconsciously perform a cognition sufficient to classify them so that we maintain some sort of order and orientation even as we go about experiencing the myriad variety of our presentational experience.

Much of the appeal of the novel form must, I believe, come from the realization that fiction is a valid symbolic formulation of experience, functioning to give a more adequate account of the way human experience actually unfolds, not when it is merely known about or "understood," but when it is experienced in the course of human living. In the novel, as in life, presented scene follows presented scene. In the novel, the scenes are ordered, of course, not haphazard, because they are informed with artistic purpose. Consider the presentational scenes that make up the daily round of experience for Faulkner's Benjy in *The Sound and the Fury*. The thirty-three-year-old idiot experiences the conglomeration of disparate experience which comprises his restricted world, without sufficient congitive power to classify and relate the ever-changing shapes and events that continue to register upon his consciousness. But even Benjy has some powers of abstraction. In some vague way those experiences which remind him of his sister, Caddy, who is most central to his life, are integrated in his mind. The integration is initiated by a cognition, which itself springs from Benjy's values. The reader, once aware of Benjy's pathetic situation as an adult idiot who possesses a touching, however limited, sensibility, follows the main line of the action—seeing the world as Benjy sees it, a confused welter of kaleidoscopic experiences, having meaning only as they are related to his vague memory and longing for his sister, the only one, with the exception of Dilsey, who responds to Benjy as an individual human being. When we examine an early episode from the Benjy section of the novel, we see that Benjy's existence without Caddy is intolerable for him, and we see that the attitude of the family is directly related to his state of existence:

Versh put my overshoes and overcoat on and we took my cap and went out. Uncle Maury was putting the bottle away in the sideboard in the dining-room.

"Keep him out about half an hour, boy." Uncle Maury said. "Keep him in the yard, now."

"Yes, sir." Versh said. "We don't never let him get off the place."

We went out doors. The sun was cold and bright.

"Where you heading for." Versh said. "You don't think you going to town, does you." We went through the rattling leaves. The gate was cold. "You better keep them hands in your pockets," Versh said, "You get them froze onto that gate, then what you do. Whyn't you wait for them in the house." He put my hands into my pockets. I could hear him rattling in the leaves. I could smell the cold. The gate was cold.

"Here are some hickeynuts. Whooey. Git up that tree. Look here at this squirl, Benjy."

I couldn't feel the gate at all, but I could smell the bright cold.

"You better put them hands back in your pockets."

Caddy was walking. Then she was running, her booksatchell swinging and jouncing behind her.

"Hello, Benjy." Caddy said. She opened the gate and came in and stooped down. Caddy smelled like leaves. "Did you come to meet me," she said. "Did you come to meet Caddy. What did you let him get his hands so cold for, Versh."

"I told him to keep them in his pockets." Versh said. Holding onto that ahun gate."

"Did you come to meet Caddy," she said, rubbing my hands. "What is it. What are you tring to tell Caddy." Caddy smelled like trees and like when she says we were asleep.

What are you moaning about, Luster said. You can watch them again when we get to the branch. Here. Here's you a jimson weed. He gave me the flower. We went through the fence, into the lot.

"What is it." Caddy said. "What are you trying to tell Caddy. Did they send him out, Versh."

"Couldn't keep him in." Versh said. "He kept on until they let him go and he come right straight down here, looking through the gate."

"What is it." Caddy said. "Did you think it would be Christmas when I came home from school. Is that what you thought. Christmas is the day after to-morrow. Santy Clause, Benjy. Santy Claus. Come on, let's run to the house and get warm." She took my hand and we ran through the bright rustling leaves. We ran up the steps and out of the bright cold, into the dark cold.

What is most significant in the episode is the contrast in the way Benjy is regarded on the one hand by his bodyguards—Versh, Luster, and the members of the Compson family—and on the other by Caddy. For all but Caddy, Benjy is something less than a human being. His anticipation as he awaits Caddy's return from school is objectified most effectively by his clutching the iron gate. We see that if it were not for his sister, his spiritual imprisonment would be complete. For all but Caddy he is merely a care, a concern, an object to be manipulated. But when we read the work closely, Caddy is recognized as one so capable of love that it is she who grants Benjy his individual being, who gives him the acceptance which he must have for what he is. That is, for Caddy, Benjy is not a concept. Thus, when the informed reader is confronted with Benjy's experience, the scenes of life as Benjy experiences them, the formulation is fiction of great significance. The integrating principle is love, Caddy's for Benjy, and the ironic justification of Benjy's value judgment concerning his sister gives a new dimension to literary experience, a new knowledge in a new form. For social, external purposes, Caddy is seen ultimately as a fallen woman, driven by misshapen values toward a life of prostitution. But through Faulkner's unique fictional technique we are made aware of the validity of Benjy's judgment about his sister, however unexpressed as a judgment. That is, were it not for seeing her through Benjy's responses, we could not experience the realization that Caddy, whatever else she may be judged to be, is also a saint.

Form in fiction is an embodiment of meaning, just as it is in poetry, not merely a framework for content. In Ransom's ontological sense, a work is made up of many *forms*, large and small, some structural, some imagistic, some ethical, all testifying to the truth so essential to the theory of Kant and Coleridge that man experiences his life concretely through his imaging faculty, as well as abstractly through his conceptualizing one.

The essays in practical criticism which follow represent an attempt to apply the theoretical principles and convictions of a formalist criticism of fiction. What is presented is not so much a method as an approach, not so much a technique as a way of regarding the fictional work—a way suggested by John Crowe Ransom, clearly the father of formalist criticism in America. Ransom's critical practice follows directly from his *way of regarding* the poem:

> [The] subject-matter [of poetry] may be differentiated with respect to its ontology or the reality of its being. An excellent variety of critical doctrine arises recently out of this differentiation, and thus perhaps criticism leans upon ontological analysis as it was meant to do by Kant (*The World's Body*, p. 111).

For Ransom "the reality of [the poem's] being" had its distinctive representation in the image, which he viewed as functioning to imitate the "texture" or bodiness that the concrete qualitative world of man's experience possesses. And his critical focus was on the image, on those "devices of concretion" which accomplished the "miraculism" of transforming language into poetry.

In fiction as well as poetry, the ontology or reality of its being as a symbolic form suggests the approach criticism must take. Since the essential power of the fictional work resides in its *texture*, in the *forms* through which the artist constructs and relates his scenes and episodes, criticism becomes a matter of consciousness, of bringing to awareness the nondiscursive meaning embodied in the presentational units. Character, action, world, must as in poetry be concretely presented. But what makes the fictional form unique is its imitation of the way we encounter life's experience, as a succession of presentations to which we provide some integration, sometimes only to maintain orientation, sometimes to give meaning and even value to the events that pass over consciousness. But just as knowledge of life's "presentations" is a process of becoming aware—of providing a meaningful abstraction in a concept of our experience—so, too, knowledge of literature's "presentations" is a repetition of the same process. Criticism of art as well as of life is consciousness after experience; it is the discovery of meaning in a presentation.

There is nothing new, of course, in such a critical practice. Eliseo Vivas called his recent book of criticism *Creation and Discovery*, suggesting the distinct roles of the artist and critic. Or again, W. K. Wimsatt in his *The Verbal Icon* concluded: "The verbal object and its analysis constitute the domain of literary criticism."

2

Joyce's "The Dead"

In the criticism of Joyce's works, the problem of meaning is admittedly complex. In the *Dubliners* stories and in *A Portrait of the Artist*, the simple reduction to paraphrase is seldom offered by the critics, for the simple reason that there seems to be little need for paraphrase. These works, it is felt, have their own kind of complexity, but they are seldom obscure. On the other hand in *Ulysses* and *Finnegans Wake* the reduction to paraphrase is quite obviously a necessary step in the overall critical process. But it is when criticism becomes merely paraphrase, when the reduced version is accepted, however unconsciously, for the embodied meaning in the formal presentation that distortion of the work occurs. The problem for poetry criticism was clarified some twenty years ago by Cleanth Brooks in his now famous essay on the subject, "The Heresy of the Paraphrase." It is perhaps fitting that the problem for the criticism of fiction should arise with Joyce, since this "consummate master of literary form" has given us the most complex and most obscure fiction we have had. And it is also interesting that the very problems faced by a formalist criticism of poetry should arise with the extension of formalist criticism to fiction. Both Cleanth Brooks and Bernard Benstock make the same critical charge and for the same underlying reasons; both speak for the integrity of the kind of meaning embodied in literary forms.

In summing up the exegetic accounts of *Finnegans Wake*, Benstock writes:

> Already available to the lay reader and the scholar are a "Skeleton Key," a "census," a "reading of *Finnegans Wake*," a "concordance" (and a "dictionary" is in the offing), as well as book-length studies of literary allusions, religious significance, songs and "structure and motif" in the *Wake*. Articles in scholarly publications and commentaries in popular periodicals abound. . . . Yet many of the most basic questions (especially that nagging all-inclusive one asked by the layest of lay readers: "But what is it all about exactly?) remain unanswered.
>
> The basic question can well remain unanswered. William York Tindall contends that *Finnegans Wake* is about *Finnegans Wake* and I for one am content to let it go at that.

Then, in what seems a prophetic turn of events in the history of criticism, Benstock echoes Brooks's charge of "the heresy of the paraphrase":

> Here in the flesh is that digest reader who pathetically requests a paraphrase of *Finnegans Wake*, and it is equally pathetic to note how many critics and commentators seem perfectly willing to provide some sort of "pony." When the mutilated version of *Ulysses* was being printed in the United States in 1927, some 167 international literary personages banded together to protest vigorously. Perhaps some such group should now assemble to attest once and for always that a work of literary art *cannot be paraphrased*, since paraphrase is a method of reducing a work into something else, and in the case of the *Wake* it most often proves to be reducing toward absurdity.
>
> The only worthwhile method of explicating the *Wake* is through augmentation, not diminution.[1]

Like Brooks, Benstock deplores the implicit assumption that seems to underlie the "lay readers'" question—the assumption that the paraphrase is an adequate representation of the work or even equal to it in meaning. I cite Benstock's vehement comments on the matter because underlying them is also one of the most fundamental convictions of the formalist critic, namely that the work of art formulates a complexity of meaning which cannot be formulated in conceptual prose statements.

Yet we must not be too hasty in dismissing that "basic question" asked by the "layest of lay readers": "But what is it all about exactly?" It may be understandingly dismissed if it is understood in Benstock's sense to request a facile conceptual representation which the questioner naïvely believes will stand for what is given in the work. On another level and with a sophisticated questioner, not a *"lay"* questioner, one like Wayne Booth, for example, the question cannot be put aside with *"Finnegans Wake* is about *Finnegans Wake."* And Booth asks the question not only of *Finnegans Wake* and even of *Ulysses* but, before he has finished, of *Portrait* as well: "Except for occasional outbursts of bravado nobody has ever claimed that Joyce is clear. In all the skeleton Keys and classroom guides there is an open assumption that his later works, *Ulysses* and *Finnegans Wake,* cannot be read; they can only be studied." [2] And again:

> It is fine to know that in *Ulysses* Stephen stands in some way for Telemachus and Bloom for his wandering father, Ulysses. But it would also be useful to know whether the work is comic or tragic, or if it a combination, where the elements fall. Can two readers be said to have read the same book if one thinks it ends affirmatively and the other sees the ending as pessimistic? [3]

Booth's question is a radical one for criticism. The formalist would answer, I believe, that only two possibilities are present: either the work is incomplete and thereby a failure as an artistic work, or criticism is incomplete and has failed to provide a reading of the work sufficiently sensitive to establish a statement of the work's "logical core."

If the fault lies in Joyce's art, it would necessarily be the direct result of the artist's failure to embody in his work an interpretation of the experiences he has presented. T. M. Greene is quite to the point when he writes "a work of art expresses the artist's *interpretation* of a given subject-matter." [4] The italicized word is his doing, not mine. For the formalist, an artistic presentation of experience that does not embody at the same time an artistic judgment is incomplete as an artistic work. That is, the mere formal organization of subject matter without an interpretation, however subtley embodied, is at best an *aesthetic*, not an *artistic*, presentation. Booth considers one other possibility, and rejects it, namely that Joyce's book in presenting a successful imitation of the ambiguity of experience is thereby itself necessarily ambiguous: "It is really no explanation to say that Joyce has succeeded in imitating life so well that like life itself his books seem totally ambiguous, totally open to whatever interpretation the reader wants to place on them." [5] One must agree with Booth! To present human experience as "ambiguous" must not be to present an ambiguous book. The presentation of life as "ambiguous" is, of course, an "interpretation." And if it is the "interpretation" of the artist it must be incorporated in the work as his embodied artistic judgment. As Kant says: "The combination and harmony of both cognitive faculties, Sensibility and Understanding, which cannot dispense with one another, but which yet cannot well be united without constraint and mutual prejudice, must appear to be undesigned and so to be brought about by themselves: otherwise it is not *beautiful art.*" [6]

On the other hand if the fault lies in the critic's reading of the work, then the failure must be ascribed to Joycean criticism. The charge that the work is obscure or ambiguous will not justify the critic's inability to provide a reading that will do justice to a work which has been affirmed by readers universally to be one of the great books of its time. It would not be the first time that criticism lagged far behind the judgment of sensitive readers. *Moby Dick* was considered worthwhile for its account of whaling lore but not as a great work until some sixty years after its publication. Similarly *Huckleberry Finn*, hardly an obscure work for modern readers, was nevertheless read as a boys' adventure story, but one so inelegant as to be banned from the schoolroom. T. S. Eliot's *The Waste Land* was first presented to me by that formidable critic, the literature teacher, as being a naturalistic and totally pessimistic account of modern man. Only later with the sensitive and coherent reading of Cleanth Brooks was it seen as essentially a religious poem and ultimately optimistic in its presentation of man. Unfortunately criticism does not precede judgment of a work's worth. By definition, criticism for the formalist is the consciousness that follows the experience of the work; on the other hand value judgment is first a response, one that is later articulated in criticism, but one belonging to all sensitive readers. Having been affirmed by a half century of readers, *Ulysses* can afford to wait for the consciousness that is criticism. The critic's task is also a responsibility. He can only follow the advice that Faulkner gave to the student at Virginia who asked of *The Sound and the Fury*, "But Mr. Faulkner, what do I do if I *have* read it a second time and I still don't understand it?" And Faulkner replied, "Read it again, and then read it again."

But the most damning questions for either Joyce's art or modern criticism's reading of it are asked in quite specific detail by Booth about Joyce's earlier novel. Again the problem is that of cognition, of discerning the work's overall meaning, in Ransom's term the problem of the "logical core" of the work. I will quote Booth at some length:

> Rather than pursue such general questions about Joyce's admittedly difficult later works, it will be more useful to look closely at that earlier work for which no skeleton key has been thought necessary, A *Portrait of the Artist as a Young Man* (1916). Everyone seems by now agreed that it is a masterpiece in the modern mode. Perhaps we can accept it as that—indeed accept it as an unquestionably great work from any viewpoint —and still feel free to ask a few irreverent questions.
>
> The structure of this "authorless" work is based on the growth of a sensitive boy to young manhood. The steps in his growth are obviously constructed with great care. Each of the first four sections ends a period of Stephen's life with what Joyce, in an earlier draft, calls an epiphany: a peculiar revelation of the inner reality of an experience, accompanied with great elation, as in a mystical religious experience. Each is followed by the opening of a new chapter on a very prosaic, even depressed level. Now here is clearly a careful structural preparation—for what? For a transformation, or for a merely cyclical return? Is the final exaltation a release from the depressing features of Irish life which have tainted the earlier experiences? Or is it the fifth turn in an endless cycle? And in either case, is Stephen always to be viewed with the same deadly seriousness with which he views himself? Is it to artistic maturity that he grows? As the young man goes into exile from Ireland, goes "to encounter

for the millionth time the reality of experience and to forge in the smithy" of his soul "the uncreated conscience" of his race, are we to take this, with Harry Levin, as a fully serious portrait of the artist Dedalus, praying to his namesake Daedalus, to stand him "now and ever in good stead"? Or is the inflated style, as Mark Shorer tells us, Joyce's clue that the young Icarus is flying too close to the sun, with the "excessive lyric relaxation" of Stephen's final style punctuating "the illusory nature of the whole ambition"? The young man takes himself and his flight with deadly solemnity. Should we?

To see the difficulties clearly, let us consider three crucial episodes, all from the final section: his rejection of the priesthood, his exposition of what he takes to be Thomistic aesthetics, and his composition of a poem.

Is his rejection of the priesthood a triumph, a tragedy, or merely a comedy of errors? Most readers, even those who follow the new trend of reading Stephen ironically, seem to have read it as a triumph: the artist has rid himself of one of the chains that bound him. To Caroline Gordon, this is a serious misreading. "I suspect that Joyce's *Portrait* has been misread by a whole generation." She sees the rejection as "the picture of a soul that is being damned for time and eternity caught in the act of foreseeing and foreknowing its damnation," and she cites in evidence the fall of Icarus and Stephen's own statement to Cranly that he is not afraid to make a mistake, "even a great mistake, a lifelong mistake and perhaps for eternity, too." Well, which *Portrait* do we choose, that of the artistic soul battling through successfully to his necessary freedom, or that of the child of God, choosing, like Lucifer, his own damnation? No two books could be further from each other than the two we envision here. There may be a sufficient core of what is simply interesting to salvage the book as a great work of the sensibility, but unless we are willing to retreat into babbling and incommunicable relativism, we cannot believe that it is *both* a portrait of the prisoner freed *and* a portrait of the soul placing itself in chains.

Critics have had even more difficulty with Stephen's aesthetic theory, ostensibly developed from Aquinas. Is the book itself, as Grant Redford tells us, an "objectification of an artistic proposition and a method announced by the central character," achieving for Joyce the "wholeness, harmony, and radiance" that Stephen celebrates in his theory? Or is it, as Father Noon says, an ironic portrait of Stephen's immature aesthetics? Joyce wanted to qualify Stephen's utterances, Father Noon tells us, "by inviting attention to his own more sophisticated literary concerns," and he stands apart from the Thomist aesthetics, watching Stephen miss the clue in his drive for an impersonal, dramatic narration. "The comparison of the artist with the God of the creation," taken "straight" by many critics, is for Father Noon "the climax of Joyce's ironic development of the Dedalus aesthetic."

Finally, what of the precious villanelle? Does Joyce intend it to be taken as a serious sign of Stephen's artistry, as a sign of his genuine but amusingly pretentious precocity, or as something else entirely?

> *Are you not weary of ardent ways,*
> *Lure of the fallen seraphim?*
> *Tell no more of enchanted days.*
>
> *Your eyes have set man's heart ablaze*
> *And you have had your will of him.*
> *Are you not weary of ardent ways? . . .*

Hardly anyone has committed himself in public about the quality of this poem. Are we to smile at Stephen or pity him in his tortured longing? Are we to marvel at his artistry, or scoff at his conceit? Or are we merely to say, "How remarkable an insight into the kind of poem that would be written by an adolescent in love, if he were artistically inclined?" The poem, we are told, "enfolded him like a shining cloud, enfolded him like water with a liquid life: and like a cloud of vapour or like waters circumfluent in space the liquid letters of speech, symbols of the element of mystery, flowed forth over his brain." As we recall Jean Paul's formula for "romantic irony," "hot baths of sentiment followed by cold showers of irony," we can only ask here which tap has been turned on. Are we to swoon—or laugh? [7]

Either Wayne Booth's conclusion is accurate: "We simply cannot avoid the conclusion that the book itself is at fault, regardless of its great virtues," [8] or it is inaccurate, in which case it is the critic's responsibility to put the reader on the right track; to provide a statement of the work's "logical core" which will render the work available to the reader. If these works of Joyce are affirmed to be successful artistic presentations, then the cognitive element necessarily present in each presentation must be discerned by the critic; it is, to use R. P. Blackmur's phrase, the "critic's job of work." Wayne Booth has, I believe, raised a most serious question in Joycean criticism.

For the formalist critic, the answers to Booth's questions must come from the close reading of the work's "texture." Ransom meant by the term the concrete presentations of the poem, primarily the image taken in its broadest sense of being the poem's basic unit of concretion. As has been suggested, in fiction the form that

the basic unit of texture takes is the scene, which functions ontologically in the same way that the image
functions in the poem, namely as an embodied presentation of meaning. The analogy can, I believe, be continued further: just as the poem itself is finally to be
viewed as one overall single image, i.e., one concrete
presentation, so also a fictional work may be viewed
as a single concrete presentation made up of episodes
which in turn are composed of scenes. I mean to suggest by the term "episode" that unit of dramatic expressive meaning which may be formulated by an
event, or situation, or action, or a relationship between
characters or an objectification of a character's state of
mind, which is integral to the work as a whole, but
which is distinguishable as a separate unit of presentational meaning. A formalist analysis of fiction must, I
believe, require a conscious awareness of these building
segments that contribute to the work's presentational
immediacy and dramatic structure. The real heresy in
reading fiction is, I think, an underlying belief that one
is, after all, reading prose. As a former professor of mine
declared to the class, "I don't see why you're so concerned about reading literature; it's just the English
language." He was wrong, of course, and the students
were justified in their apprehensiveness. For what one
is reading in a fictional scene is more nearly analogous
to viewing a painting than to comprehending a paragraph of a prose text. And the experiencing of a novel is
closer ontologically, I think, to listening to a musical
presentation than it is to reading a book of conceptual
prose. Finally, for the formalist critic, each concrete
presentation must be viewed in the light of its function
in the overall single image which is the work.

Yet Wayne Booth's charge that *Portrait* is a failure is
itself a kind of failure in criticism—in reading the
meaning through form that the novel represents. In

Joyce's "The Dead" the problem of the meaning of the various scenes that constitute the Misses Morkan's party would undoubtedly be a serious one and open to the same charge that Booth's brings to *Portrait*. But "The Dead" has the final episode of Gabriel's awakening which acts to condition the meaning of the earlier episodes, so that we proceed with much more confidence in examining the formal presentations which constitute the long first part of the work. But we also proceed with the conviction that it is precisely in the devices of his formal presentation, in those indirections of discourse which constitute his fictional style, that Joyce's meaning resides. And the preoccupation with form, then, becomes in reality a preoccupation with meaning.

When we read Eliot's *The Waste Land* today we wonder how we could have assented to the critics who called its meaning obscure. Eliot's speaker, however changeable from section to section, nevertheless spoke with a consistent and recognizable irony that left no doubt about meaning: The "crowd" that "flowed over London bridge" is explained in an immediate utterance: "So many, I had not thought death had undone so many." Add to the speaker's reflective assertion the suggested meanings which attend the allusion to Dante's Inferno, and meaning becomes so direct as to be nearly didactic. Against the backdrop of such direct presentations there is no problem in reading a section like "The Game of Chess," in which the two cockney women in the pub in the mere expression of their everyday concerns express also the spiritual sterility of Eliot's land of the dead.

But Joyce's story "The Dead" is much more subtle. There is no ironic sensibility that comments on the action, and there is no allusion to give connotative assurance that one is on the right track. Joyce offers his presentations without direct or indirect supports to cognition. And finally, I think that we feel that Joyce's is the more successful art.

"The Dead" is certainly one of the masterpieces in the Joyce canon. Its themes, recognizably present in the later works, are embodied in a much more direct manner of presentation: the theme of spiritual death, of spiritual rebirth, and the theme of the freedom of the human spirit as a necessary condition for living and loving. It would be folly for the critic of whatever persuasion not to grant that a sound reading of "The Dead" is an obvious prerequisite to the reading of Joyce's later works. I would like to examine some scenes and episodes from the first half of the story which is intended to suggest the way Joyce has built his meanings to a climactic embodiment in the second half.

When we examine the opening episode, in the light of the work itself taken as one large presentation, one major contrast with subsequent episodes immediately emerges: the opening episode is an *objective* presentation of the world of the action. That is, here is the way the world actually is before Gabriel enters. Once Gabriel is present, the objective view diminishes, sometimes clouded by his responses, sometimes altogether distorted by its presentation through his viewpoint. The tone of the opening scene of the three-scene episode is quite different from the tone after Gabriel enters the action:

> Lily, the caretaker's daughter, was literally run off her feet. Hardly had she brought one gentleman into the little pantry behind the office on the gound floor and helped him off with his overcoat than the wheezy hall-door bell clanged again and she had to scamper along the bare hallway to let in another guest.

For the simple tastes of Lily, scurrying about her duties of greeting the guests, and for Miss Kate and Miss Julia, who "were there, gossiping and laughing and fussing," the party to come had no quality of spiritual sterility about it. Although the party was long since a ritual, "always a great affair, the Misses Morkan's annual dance," it did not occur to these sensibilities that at the same time it had become a spiritually sterile ritual. Although not evident in the opening episode, later episodes will present the gathering as the very expression of spiritual sterility. The conversation at the table just prior to Gabriel's speech is a good instance:

> The subject of talk was the opera company which was then at the Theatre Royal. Mr. Bartell D'Arcy, the tenor, a dark-complexioned young man with a smart moustache, praised very highly the leading contralto of the company but Miss Furlong thought she had a rather vulgar style of production. Freddy Malins said there was a negro chieftain singing in the second part of the Gaiety pantomime who had one of the finest voices he had ever heard.

An understanding of the scene turns on the realization that Bartell D'Arcy is not one of the spiritually dead. In contrast to Gabriel, he is presented as one who feels no compulsion to put himself forward, as Gabriel does in, for example, his annual speech, or as Mr. Browne does in his insistence on telling stories, or as Miss Furlong and Freddy Malins do in their contrary responses in this scene. They are, of course, "the dead" of the story. The point here is that with "the dead," all qualities of the real world are dissipated by subjective responses. In this scene the possibility of communication vanishes, as each participant except Bartell D'Arcy responds. (Mary Jane may also be an exception. But Mary Jane is also a victim, but of another kind. She is reminiscent of Maria in "Clay.") The conversation, about opera singers and judgments about them, becomes less a subject for conversation as the scene develops than a vehicle for the expression of judgments directed to call attention to the speaker. Mr. Browne's lengthy account of the history of the opera companies who used to come to Dublin concludes with a judgment which is also something of a challenge to the group. The responses of the participants in the conversation embody one central theme of the work: the inability to celebrate the world of objective reality is synonymous with the inability to be alive. Mr. Browne concludes: "Why did they never play the grand old operas now, he asked. *Dinorah, Lucrezia Borgia*? Because they could not get the voices to sing them: that was why." Then the objective response: " 'O, well,' said Mr. Bartell D'Arcy, 'I presume there are as good singers today as there were then.' " Now the subjective defense: " 'Where are they?' asked Mr. Browne defiantly." And the answer is recognizable as objectively real: " 'In London, Paris, Milan,' said Mr. Bartell D'Arcy warmly. 'I suppose Caruso, for example, is quite as good, if not better than any of the men you have mentioned.' " But again what is real about the subject disappears in the defensive response: " 'Maybe so,' said Mr. Browne. 'But *I* may tell you I doubt it strongly.' " And then one who in her mindlessness is not really a part of the conversation: " 'O, I'd give anything to hear Caruso sing,' said Mary Jane." Now the real is once more obscured in the response of sentimentality:

"For me," said Aunt Kate, who had been picking a bone, "there was only one tenor. To please me, I mean. But I suppose none of you have ever heard of him."

"Who was he, Miss Morkan?" asked Mr. Bartell D'Arcy politely.

"His name," said Aunt Kate, "was Parkinson. I heard him when he was in his prime and I think he had then the purest tenor voice that was ever put into a man's throat."

There is no rejection in the response of Bartell D'Arcy, simply an impulse to be objective: " 'Strange, I never even heard of him.' " But Mr. Browne seizes the opportunity to put down D'Arcy: " 'Yes, yes, Miss Morkan is right,' said Mr. Browne. 'I remember hearing of old Parkinson but he is too far back for me.' " In the final utterance the last vestige of what could have been human communication is submerged in sentimentality: " 'A beautiful, pure, sweet, mellow English tenor,' said Aunt Kate with enthusiasm." These, then, are "the dead," as fully realized and as expressionistically valid as that other famous objectification of drawing-room sterility: "In the room the women come and go/ Talking of Michaelangelo."

The theme of spiritual death dominates the entire first section of the work, which, considered from the standpoint of its ontological structure, is divided into two large presentations: the first is the party, which embodies the subject matter of "the dead"; the second is the marriage relationship between Gabriel and Gretta, which comprises the rebirth of Gabriel.

Although it is those episodes of the first section which focus specifically on Gabriel that are dominant, one other episode, focusing on Mr. Browne and Freddy Malins, also presents variations of the theme of death-in-life. When Mr. Browne arrives at the affair, he moves at once to be the center of attention. He leads the three young ladies, who have been instructed to present him to the assembled guests, into the back room where he performs dramatically as he pours himself a drink. When his performance becomes of questionable taste and is rejected by the ladies, he "turned promptly to the two young men who were more appreciative."

That is, like Freddy Malins and like Gabriel, Mr. Browne's interest is not in people, but in getting people to attend to him. Here in Joyce's presentation of Freddy Malins's entrance:

> He was laughing heartily in a high key at a story which he had been telling Gabriel on the stairs and at the same time rubbing the knuckles of his left fist backwards and forwards into his left eye.
>
> "Good evening, Freddy," said Aunt Julia.

Presently he catches sight of Mr. Browne and seizes the meeting as an opportunity for further dramatic action:

> Mr. Browne, whose face was once more wrinkling with mirth, poured out for himself a glass of whisky while Freddy Malins exploded, before he had well reached the climax of his story, in a kind of high-pitched bronchitic laughter and, setting down his un-tasted and overflowing glass, began to rub the knuckles of his left fist backwards and forward into his left eye, repeating words of his last phrase as well as his fit of laughter would allow him.

The point is, of course, that Mr. Browne's face that is "once more wrinkling with mirth" is like Freddy Malins's uncontrollable mirth and Gabriel's after-dinner speech: each carefully prepared and artfully timed.

The central focus of the long opening section which constitutes the first half of the work is on Gabriel, who throughout is presented as one quite incapable of attending to any reality, apart from his own subjective relationship to it. That is, Gabriel is presented as one who seldom sees or listens to any quality of the world external to himself, except as that quality is in some way enmeshed with his own self-interest in it. The impulse in Gabriel is presented as overwhelming the entire range and scope of his relationships with his fellow-man.

His first encounter with another is that with Lily, the maid, which occurs when he enters the house. His first communication with her, following the greeting, is the recognizable informal exchange characteristic of the acceptable mode of the occasion for two people with little in common. But the ritual which maintains distance with civility, with a minimum degree of engagement, is broken by Gabriel with his overly familiar questions. We see that he doesn't really mean his questions to Lily, that he has, however unaware of his action, adopted an air of condescension toward her and thus asserted his own superiority. He is annoyed and mildly shocked when her response is something more than an anticipated cliché. That is, it is clear that he has no real interest in Lily in spite of his questions and no wish to have his attention to her engaged in any but the most superficial manner.

> "Tell me, Lily," he said in a friendly tone, "do you still go to school?"
>
> "O no, sir," she answered. "I'm done schooling this year and more."
>
> "O, then," said Gabriel gaily, "I suppose we'll be going to your wedding one of these fine days with your young man, eh?"
>
> The girl glanced back at him over her shoulder and said with great bitterness:
>
> "The men that is now is only all palaver and what they can get out of you."
>
> Gabriel coloured, as if he felt he had made a mistake and, without looking at her, kicked off his galoshes and flicked actively with his muffler at his patent-leather shoes.

And then presently: "When he had flicked lustre into his shoes, he stood up and pulled his waistcoat down more tightly on his plump body. Then he took a coin rapidly from his pocket."

The coin, of course, is not a gift; it is a gesture which at once redefines the relationship which he intends. That is, for Gabriel, Lily is not Lily; she is the servant girl. We see that in his initial presentation of Gabriel, Joyce has worked painstakingly to establish at once that Gabriel's concern is always centered in Gabriel.

The encounter with Miss Ivors is another failure in human intercourse. Miss Ivors, who is also a teacher, is obviously impressed by Gabriel's book reviews, and attempts to engage his attention by a kind of simulated hostility. There should be no question that her seeming aggressiveness is intended irony. Joyce presents her at the outset as open, not deceptive, "a frank-mannered talkative young lady, with a freckled face and prominent brown eyes." Her charge when they take their places as dancing partners is quite obviously made in the spirit of the occasion, and her tone is unquestionably more of lighthearted banter than hostility:

> When they had taken their places she said abruptly:
> "I have a crow to pluck with you."
> "With me?" said Gabriel.
> She nodded her head gravely.
> "What is it?" asked Gabriel, smiling at her solemn manner.
> "Who is G. C.?" answered Miss Ivors, turning her eyes upon him.
> Gabriel coloured and was about to knit his brows, as if he did not understand, when she said bluntly:
> "O, innocent Amy! I have found out that you write for *The Daily Express*. Now, aren't you ashamed of yourself?"
> "Why should I be ashamed of myself?" asked Gabriel, blinking his eyes and trying to smile.

"Well, I'm ashamed of you," said Miss Ivors frankly. "To say you'd write for a paper like that. I didn't think you were a West Briton."

That Miss Ivors's intention was not to rebuke Gabriel is obvious at the point at which she realizes that he has taken her literally:

> He continued blinking his eyes and trying to smile and murmured lamely that he saw nothing political in writing reviews of books.
>
> When their turn to cross had come he was still perplexed and inattentive. Miss Ivors promptly took his hand in a warm grasp and said in a soft friendly tone:
>
> "Of course, I was only joking. Come, we cross now."

Gabriel's misunderstanding is much more than just that; it is, in reality, a rejection; and more than a rejection of Miss Ivors, who presently will leave the affair before the dinner is served, it is a rejection of *what is* in the world apart from Gabriel's distortion of it.

We see finally that Gabriel's speech, the climax of the Misses Morkan's annual party, has no validity as an expression of anything but Gabriel's calculations about what will impress his listeners and Gabriel's defensive hostility, which was inadvertently engaged by Miss Ivors's playful attempts at drawing-room irony. In one final attempt at reconciliation, Miss Ivors somewhat pathetically reveals her regret at having annoyed him:

> Gabriel tried to cover his agitation by taking part in the dance with great energy. He avoided her eyes for he had seen a sour expression on her face. But when they met in the long chain he was surprised to feel his hand firmly pressed. She looked at him from under her brows for a moment quizzically until he

> smiled. Then, just as the chain was about to start
> again, she stood on tiptoe and whispered into his ear:
> "West Briton!"

And we see that Miss Ivors is not attacking Gabriel.
She is more nearly flirting with him. It is clear that her
intention throughout was to have a conversation with
him. In her overzealous approach, she has inadvertently
offended him, because Gabriel is constitutionally unable
to attend to anyone except in relation to his own concerns. Further, her quizzical look also suggests her dismay
at not finding what she had a right to expect from another human: a living, not a deadening response. In the
following scene, Gretta enters, but Gabriel's attitude toward her is somewhat distant, and his response to her
enthusiastic proposal that they act on the suggestion of
a trip to the west of Ireland is abrupt:

> His wife clasped her hands excitedly and gave a
> little jump.
> "O, do go, Gabriel," she cried. "I'd love to see Gal-
> way again."
> "You can go if you like," said Gabriel coldly.

What we see emphasized in the scene is one instance in
which Gabriel's relationship with his wife is distorted
because he is incapable of attending to her as she is.
Like a child he is still caught up in his hostile feelings
for Miss Ivors. The scene, however minor, makes its con-
tribution to that climactic scene at the hotel room when
Gabriel at the outset is once again dead to any objectively real relationship with his wife and for similar
reasons.

Gabriel's misconception of Miss Ivors's remarks has
another significant ramification in its effect on the subject matter of Gabriel's speech, one which further contributes to the character of the speech itself. He contrives
a theme which has its basis in his desire to vent his

hostility. The validity of what he would say was of little concern; what he would say involved using Aunt Kate and Aunt Julia for his carefully calculated purposes:

> He would say, alluding to Aunt Kate and Aunt Julia: "Ladies and Gentlemen, the generation which is now on the wane among us may have had its faults but for my part I think it had certain qualities of hospitality, of humour, of humanity, which the new and very serious and hypereducated generation that is growing up around us seems to me to lack." Very good: that was one for Miss Ivors. What did he care that his aunts were only two ignorant old women?

And we see that Gabriel's characteristic defensiveness and hostility function finally in the same way that his annual practice of using the Misses Morkan's party as a vehicle to project himself as the center of attention functions: each celebrates the self at the expense of the qualitative existence of the real world. In Joyce's presentation of the Misses Morkan's drawing-room world, it is just such a rejection of the real that is the chief characteristic of "the dead."

One moment of awakening does occur both for Gabriel and for the participants at the party: the excellent performance by Aunt Julia. The little incident establishes the latent potential for living that does still exist in the gathering and especially in Gabriel. Joyce is precise in the embodied theme of the presentation:

> Gabriel recognized the prelude. It was that of an old song of Aunt Julia's—*Arrayed for the Bridal.* Her voice, strong and clear in tone, attacked with great spirit the runs which embellish the air and though she sang very rapidly she did not miss even the smallest of the grace notes. To follow the voice, without looking at the singer's face, was to feel and share the excite-

ment of swift and secure flight. Gabriel applauded loudly with all the others at the close of the song and loud applause was borne in from the invisible supper table. It sounded so genuine that a little colour struggled into Aunt Julia's face.

This celebration of an objectively real quality of the world external to the self is, however, short-lived. Freddy Malins seizes the moment for his own interests, and the dead once more obliterate the living:

Freddy Malins, who had listened with his head perched sideways to hear her better, was still applauding when everyone else had ceased and talking animatedly to his mother who nodded her head gravely and slowly in acquiescence. At last, when he could clap no more, he stood up suddenly and hurried across the room to Aunt Julia whose hand he seized and held in both his hands, shaking it when words failed him or the catch in his voice proved too much for him.

But presently Freddy Malins is thrust aside by that other master of attention-getting:

Mr. Browne extended his open hand towards her and said to those who were near him in the manner of a showman introducing a prodigy to an audience:
"Miss Julia Morkan, my latest discovery."

As readers we readily discern the nature of the difference between the performances of Aunt Julia and presently Bartell D'Arcy on the one hand and the performances of Freddy Malins, Mr. Browne, and Gabriel in his speech on the other. It is, of course, a necessary discernment for the reading of the work.

Near the close of the long first part, two significant episodes underscore Gabriel's inability to be present to the real world around him, which in Joyce quite clearly means to be alive to it: the first is Gabriel's total failure to comprehend why Miss Ivors is leaving the party.

> On the landing outside the drawing room Gabriel found his wife and Mary Jane trying to persuade Miss Ivors to stay for supper. But Miss Ivors, who had put on her hat and was buttoning her cloak, would not stay. She did not feel in the least hungry and she had already overstayed her time.

Mary Jane reveals a vague awareness of Miss Ivors's reason for leaving the party: " 'I am afraid you didn't enjoy yourself at all,' said Mary Jane hopelessly." But Gabriel's response reveals that he is completely insensitive to Miss Ivors's feelings and completely oblivious to his own part in her withdrawal: " 'If you will allow me, Miss Ivors, I'll see you home if you are really obliged to go.' " And, again, after her dismay, which is followed by her "abrupt departure," Gabriel's reflections reveal his inability to participate in the objective reality of any human situation. We see him virtually imprisoned within a world created by his own distorted vision: "Gabriel asked himself was he the cause of her abrupt departure. But she did not seem to be in ill humour: she had gone away laughing. He stared blankly down the staircase." Viewed externally, Gabriel seems to be alive to his world: a scholar who "had taken his degree in the Royal University," and now a writer of reviews for the *Daily Express* and a teacher in the college. But with our insight into his internal world we see that he is quite dead to what is most real in his intercourse with other humans. His specific failure is presented as his characteristic inability to be present to the present. The second episode of the long first section is Gabriel's false speech to the assemblage, which comes to a climax in his praise of the Misses Morkan as "the Three Graces of the Dublin musical world." What makes the speech false from beginning to end is centered in the realization that it is not an honest assertion of an individual self, but the projection of a masked self: "As long as this one roof shelters the good ladies aforesaid—and I wish from my heart it may do so for many and many a long year to come" . . . etc. We remember that what hangs over his pronouncements is an earlier one spoken to himself: "What did he care that his aunts were only two ignorant old women."

It is in the light of our understanding of the presentations of the first part of the work that our reading of the second, the climax of the rebirth epiphany, can best be read. It begins with Gabriel's rapt attention on Gretta who is standing at the top of the stair: "She was leaning on the bannisters, listening to something. Gabriel was surprised at her stillness and strained his ear to listen also." Here is his first celebration of a present reality after the Aunt Julia playing scene: "If he were a painter, he would paint her in that attitude." Presently what is Gretta becomes lost again, this time in his seeing her as the object of his sexual interest and gratification: "He could have flung his arms about her hips and held her still, for his arms were trembling with desire to seize her and only the stress of his nails against the palms of his hands held the wild impulse of his body in check."

It is this anticipation of the forthcoming sexual encounter that blinds him once again to what is real about his wife's mood. The conversation which he directs to her at this point becomes as false as his earlier after-dinner speech. He introduces the story of Freddy Malins's returning money which Gabriel had loaned him and compliments Freddy, which is quite the opposite of his real being at the moment: "Gabriel strove to restrain himself from breaking out into brutal language about the sottish Malins and his pound." The marriage relationship, which is the chief subject matter of the story's second part, is now distorted by his confused attempt to communicate with her: ostensibly concerning Freddy Malins (and that falsely) but really concerning his sexual desires. The point is that Gabriel is presented as needing to calculate his responses, with the result that he masks his real feelings, and there is no real communication. There is a fine irony in Gretta's response: "Then, suddenly raising herself on tiptoe and resting her hands lightly on his shoulders, she kissed him. 'You are a very generous person, Gabriel,' she said." That is, she praises him for his caring about Freddy Malins because she has taken what he says as real. And the distortion of their communion in their spiritual marriage is as complete as the distortion and confusion of their physical relationship.

> Gabriel, trembling with delight at her sudden kiss and at the quaintness of her phrase, put his hands on her hair and began smoothing it back, scarcely touching it with his fingers. The washing had made it fine and brilliant. His heart was brimming over with happiness. Just when he was wishing it she had come to him of her own accord. Perhaps her thoughts had been running with his. Perhaps she had felt the impetuous desire that was in him, and then the yielding mood had come upon her. Now that she had fallen to him so easily, he wondered why he had been so diffident.

And we see that for Gabriel, Gretta is not Gretta, she is his conquest. In this respect the order of his relationship to Gretta is closer to that of his relationship with Miss Ivors and earlier with Lily than it is to a marriage relationship.

The climax in the presentation of the distortion occurs when he asks, "Gretta, dear, what are you thinking about?"—expecting, of course, just one answer. Her answer that she is thinking about the song, "The Lass of Aughrim," is the first shock in the process of his return to the realm of the living. Joyce's device of the mirror image of Gabriel is one of the most effective presentations in the story. The mirror functions as the first step in the whole process of Gabriel's rebirth; it is the self confronting the self in a revelation which had heretofore never been consummated: "Gabriel stood stock-still for a moment in astonishment and them followed her. As he passed in the way of the cheval-glass he caught sight of himself in full length, his broad, well-filled shirt front, the face whose expression always puzzled him when he saw it in a mirror."

Her answer when he presses to know her concern merely intensifies his anger, and his masked feelings begin to show: " 'Someone you were in love with?' he asked ironically." The irony reflects his complete inability to see her and the way she feels. Joyce's subject matter, we realize, has been the complex relationship between living and loving. Gabriel here is still one of the dead in his inability to grant the independent being of another. But consistent with her character as one who is nowhere indirect, Gretta misses the irony of his question. Her answer is a candid revelation of herself: " 'It was a young boy I used to know,' she answered, 'named Michael Furey.' " Gabriel's response on the other hand intensifies the embodiment of Joyce's theme. His is at once the calculated response: "Gabriel was silent. He did not wish her to think that he was interested in this delicate boy." For Gabriel, in his present being as one of the spiritually dead, there is no possibility of accepting what is her real concern. " 'What was he?' asked Gabriel still ironically. 'He was in the gasworks,' she said."

In the light of the final scene in which Gabriel is

shocked into his first real undistorted view of himself
as not merely one of the assembled dead but one who
played a leading role in carrying out their ritual, each
scene and episode that constituted the party is singularly unambiguous in meaning. We see that it is not
merely the banality of their concerns and preoccupations
which define what it means to be a participant in the
rituals of the dead. And even their characteristic inability to comprehend the real existence of the world
apart from the self does not finally differentiate those
whom Joyce presents as the dead. We see that they are
unfree to respond in any but their own narrow pattern
of response. Each is an imprisoned victim, alternately
asserting and defending a self which he seems to have
no contact with or awareness of. The result is a kind of
spiritual hell from which only Gabriel, precisely because
of his sudden consciousness of himself as a total failure,
becomes free. And Gabriel's failure, which finally he
himself realizes, has been a failure in his humanity. It is
at this point that Gabriel is shocked into the objectivity
that characterizes the world of the living.

> Gabriel felt humiliated by the failure of his irony and
> by the evocation of this figure from the dead, a boy in
> the gasworks. While he had been full of memories
> of their secret life together, full of tenderness and joy
> and desire, she had been comparing him in her mind
> with another. A shameful consciousness of his own
> person assailed him. He saw himself as a ludicrous
> figure, acting as a pennyboy for his aunts, a nervous,
> well-meaning sentimentalist, orating to vulgarians
> and idealising his clownish lusts, the pitiable fatuous
> fellow he had caught a glimpse of in the mirror.
> Instinctively he turned his back more to the light lest
> she might see the shame that burned upon his fore-
> head.

It is from this new condition of his being that Gabriel can attend to his wife. And when she reveals herself, he for the first time can hear her speak. The scene marks the first real moment in the evolution of their reborn marriage: "He did not question her again, for he felt that she would tell him of herself. Her hand was warm and moist: it did not respond to his touch, but he continued to caress it just as he had carressed her first letter to him that spring morning."

There is no rejection of his humanity in the dénouement following his awakening. The final episode presents a rapid series of Gabriel's new responses; they are a direct contrast to the responses of "the dead." When he attends to Gretta, it is Gretta that is his concern: "She stopped, choking with sobs, and, overcome by emotion, flung herself face downward on the bed, sobbing in the quilt. Gabriel held her hand for a moment longer, irresolutely, and then, shy of intruding on her grief, let it fall gently and walked quietly to the window." In this first response which follows Gabriel's new vision of the world, the formal presentations now all embody a new thematic meaning: they present what it means to belong to the world of the living. When Gabriel sees that Gretta had, in the midst of his comforting, fallen asleep, his response is in direct contrast to his earlier self-concern:

> Gabriel, leaning on his elbow, looked for a few moments unresentfully on her tangled hair and half-open mouth, listening to her deep-drawn breath. So she had had that romance in her life: a man had died for her sake. It hardly pained him now to think how poor a part he, her husband, had played in her life. He watched her while she slept, as though he and she had never lived together as man and wife.

It is here that we realize that Gabriel's relationship to his wife has undergone a radical change. It is here that we realize that for Joyce one meaning of being able to love is being able to attend to the object with the kind of attention that wishes to know it as fully as possible: "His curious eyes rested long upon her face and on her hair: and, as he thought of what she must have been then, in that time of her first girlish beauty, a strange, friendly pity for her entered his soul." Throughout the scene Gabriel's love for his wife is presented as more realistic than romantic, given to matter-of-factness rather than to sentimentality: "He did not like to say even to himself that her face was no longer beautiful, but he knew that it was no longer the face for which Michael Furey had braved death."

It is clear that the singular result of Gabriel's new ability to live resides in his being able to love. But it is not merely Gabriel's love for his wife that marks his new state of being; his new-found capacity extends to those of his immediate world. As his reflection turns to the party, to what he now sees as "his own foolish speech," suddenly into his consciousness comes a new image of his aunts:

> Poor Aunt Julia! She too would soon be a shade with the shade of Patrick Morkan and his horse. He had caught that haggard look upon her face for a moment when she was singing *Arrayed for the Bridal*. Soon, perhaps, he would be sitting in that same drawing room, dressed in black, his silk hat on his knees. The blinds would be drawn down and Aunt Kate would be sitting beside him, crying and blowing her nose and telling him how Julia had died. He would cast about in his mind for some words that might console her, and he would find only lame and useless ones. Yes, yes: that would happen very soon.

Joyce, that "consummate master of form," brings together in this scene thematic presentations which have been expressed earlier but with different connotative meaning: Aunt Julia's singing had been a moment of living in the world of the dead. For Gabriel it was his one moment of attending: "To follow the voice, without looking at the singer's face, was to feel and share the excitement of swift and secure flight. Gabriel applauded loudly with all the others." But now it is clear that in his one instance of being present to another, Gabriel had indeed been "looking at the singer's face": "He had caught that haggard look upon her face for a moment when she was singing *Arrayed for the Bridal.*" The point is that in the earlier instance, the single presentation of *the living* in the midst of *the dead*, Joyce had presented Gabriel as merely responding to Aunt Julia's singing with applause. Not only had no significance been attached to his vision of "that haggard look," the vision itself had not even risen to consciousness. The contrast marks by stylistic omission the experienced difference between the thematic embodiment of "the dead" and that of "the living." Again the associations accompanying that earlier explosive utterance, "What did he care that his aunts were only two ignorant old women?" reverberate ironically in this passage. That is, it is in his new state of being capable of *caring* that makes possible Gabriel's vision of Aunt Julia arrayed, not for "the bridal" but for the burial. A further irony is evident in Gabriel's present inarticulateness in contrast to his earlier facility to rise to any occasion.

But the central irony resides in the way Joyce works with the theme of death. In an earlier presentation of the ritual of the dead, Mr. Browne and Mary Jane inadvertently come to an expression in their facile drawing-room conversation of the work's central theme. When Mr. Browne, who is "of the other persuasion," questions the practice of the monks in sleeping in their coffins rather than in "a comfortable spring bed," Mary Jane dutifully, however unconsciously, provides an explanation: " 'The coffin,' said Mary Jane, 'is to remind them of their last end.' "

Further, one of the central themes which Gabriel has chosen for his speech, and again in the context of presentation of the dead, is the theme of death. Here, of course, the assertion of the fact of death as a reality in the history of the community is ironic in the light of Gabriel's ultimate realization of death. In his speech his intention is focused solely on directing the emotions of his hearers. He does not have to "cast about in his mind" for words. His images are clichés and his rhetoric empty. The passage, however, conditions the climax of the work:

> "[let us] still cherish in our hearts the memory of those dead and gone great ones whose fame the world will not willingly let die."
>
> "Hear, hear!" said Mr. Browne loudly.
>
> "But yet," continued Gabriel, his voice falling into a softer inflection, "there are always in gatherings such as this sadder thoughts that will recur to our minds: thoughts of the past, of youth, of changes, of absent faces that we miss here tonight. Our path through life is strewn with many such sad memories; and were we to brood upon them always we could not find the heart to go on bravely with our work among the living."

As it is presented in Gabriel's speech, the realization of death is a cliché of the drawing room. The contrast with Gabriel's final realization of death and the meaning of death completes the essential contrast that gives the work its thematic structure, its meaning through its form. In the final scene Gabriel's mind goes back to the party, but now with an objective vision, one freed of the imprisonment which had blocked and distorted his being able to live. It is at this point that "The Dead" becomes another kind of symbol, at first a realistic symbol of what is universally true about human existence: "The air of the room chilled his shoulders. He stretched himself cautiously along under the sheets and lay down beside his wife. One by one they were all becoming shades." But presently Gabriel's experience of death becomes associated with his reflections on the meaning of living: "Better pass boldly into that other world, in the full glory of some passion, than fade and wither dismally with age." The utterance is presented not so much as a reasoned conclusion but as a sudden response—a response that establishes Gabriel's real, because experienced, relationship to death. It is an affirmation of living as its own justification for human existence.

Then in the same pattern of the sudden juxtaposition of continuing awarenesses, Gabriel's thoughts turn to his wife and her relationship to her dead lover:

> He thought of how she who lay beside him had locked in her heart for so many years that image of her lover's eyes when he had told her that he did not wish to live.
>
> Generous tears filled Gabriel's eyes. He had never felt like that himself towards any woman, but he knew that such a feeling must be love.

The point is, of course, not Gabriel's judgment on the validity of his wife's lover's protestations but on Gabriel's concern with Gretta's state of mind in living with her secret. Whatever the lover's feeling may be, it is quite obvious that it is Gabriel's feelings that "must be love."

Joyce's dénouement continues this theme; namely the caring for and recognition of the dead becomes the final step in the actualization of human love. In his rebirth Gabriel is presented as not merely responding to the universe of man; Gabriel's response here expands to a celebration of a larger universe:

His soul had approached that region where dwell the vast hosts of the dead. He was conscious of, but could not apprehend, their wayward and flickering existence. His own identity was fading out into a grey impalpable world: the solid world itself, which these dead had one time reared and lived in, was dissolving and dwindling.

The snow, which had been merely a realistic detail in the opening episode, becomes during the unpleasantness attending Miss Ivors's imagined attack a symbol for a place of refuge for Gabriel's withdrawal from that unpleasantness. Then in the final scene the snow image again reflects the developing theme of the work: here the snow is a symbol expressing the broader scope of Gabriel's new-found capacity for conscious awareness of man's world. In Gabriel's story, the capacity for awareness has been a prerequisite for seeing and caring for that world which is apart from his own inner concern. Now for Gabriel the snow falls through this new world —one quite different from the world of the dead which he had formerly inhabited:

> snow was general all over Ireland. It was falling on every part of the dark central plain, on the treeless hills, falling softly upon the Bog of Allen and, farther westward, softly falling into the dark mutinous Shannon waves. It was falling, too, upon every part of the lonely churchyard on the hill where Michael Furey lay buried. It lay thickly drifted on the crooked crosses and headstones, on the spears of the little gate, on the barren thorns. His soul swooned slowly as he heard the snow falling faintly through the universe and faintly falling, like the descent of their last end, upon all the living and the dead.

3

Dreiser's *Sister Carrie*

When Dreiser's first (and in many ways most successful) novel, *Sister Carrie*, is approached with the intention of discovering its particular values—just what
it is that gives it its unique power—the most immediate
impression is that of the looming presence of Dreiser
throughout the work. This is not merely the familiar
fictional device of assuming the reader's assent to his
role as an intimate go-between, as in the passage: "Before following her in her round of seeking, let us look at
the sphere in which her future was to lie." What
Dreiser does with viewpoint in *Sister Carrie* is, when
closely examined, surprisingly complex. It enables him
not merely to depict the world through the eyes of this
or that character but to infuse the novel with his own
unseen presence.

It is difficult to define what is meant by the author's
presence in the novel. Obviously, every writer makes his
presence felt in, for example, the selection of detail and
in the tone reflected by his attitude toward his material.
But Dreiser's presence is something more. From the
opening scene depicting an apprehensive Carrie de-
parting for Chicago to the final resignation from life of
a despondent Hurstwood in a Bowery flophouse, Dreiser
explains, justifies, persuades, and interprets for the
reader. Sometimes we feel his presence in the description of an action:

Whatever touch of regret at parting characterized her thoughts, it was certainly not for advantages now being given up. A gush of tears at her mother's farewell kiss, a touch in her throat when the cars clacked by in the flour mill where her father worked by the day, a pathetic sigh as the familiar green environs of the village passed in review, and the threads which bound her so lightly to girlhood and home were irretrievably broken.

Sometimes Dreiser interrupts the action in a characteristic aside:

When a girl leaves home at eighteen, she does one of two things. Either she falls into saving hands and becomes better or she rapidly assumes the cosmopolitan standard of virtue and becomes worse.

Frequently he integrates his own viewpoint with that of his characters. In the scene in which Carrie arrives at the Chicago station, the reader has been caught up in the viewpoint of Carrie for some two pages which conclude with the meeting with her sister:

"Why, how are all the folks at home?" she began; "how is father and mother?"

Carrie answered, but was looking away. Down the aisle, toward the gate leading into the waiting room and the street, stood Drouet. He was looking back. When he saw that she saw him and was safe with her sister he turned to go, sending back the shadow of a smile. Only Carrie saw it. She felt something lost to her when he moved away. When he disappeared she felt his absence thoroughly.

Then within a single statement, the first part of which could be taken as still consistent with Carrie's viewpoint, Dreiser enters the action: "With her sister she was much alone, a lone figure in a tossing, thoughtless sea." Quite obviously, it is not Carrie who views herself as "a lone figure in a tossing, thoughtless sea." And the image has a deeper function than that of suggesting Carrie's plight. It acts also to express an unnamed presence. When Carrie is moved by the sights of residential Chicago, she reflects on the meaning of happiness. But what is suggested is not merely the sensibility of a simple girl; the sensibility of another is commingled with hers. We feel the constant presence of Dreiser in the passage:

> As they drove along the smooth pavement an occasional carriage passed. She saw one stop and the footman dismount, opening the door for a gentleman who seemed to be leisurely returning from some afternoon pleasure. Across the broad lawns, now first freshening into green, she saw lamps faintly glowing upon rich interiors. Now it was but a chair, now a table, now an ornate corner, which met her eye, but it appealed to her as almost nothing else could. Such childish fancies as she had had of fairy palaces and kingly quarters now came back. She imagined across these richly carved entrance-ways, where the globed and crystalled lamps shone upon panelled doors set with stained and designed panes of glass, was neither care nor unsatisfied desire. She was perfectly certain that here was happiness.

We scarcely need to know that the quickening of excitement caused by the fleeting sight of the carriage with footman and gentleman of leisure, the "lamps faintly glowing upon rich interiors," the "ornate corner" and the "richly carved entrance-ways" is the same excitement of desire expressed in every one of Dreiser's long autobiographical accounts—we scarcely need to be reminded of such an occurrence in order to realize that here is being expressed Dreiser himself. In his portrayal of Carrie, Dreiser has not always been convincing. But ironically he has, in his depiction of Carrie, strengthened the development of the character he has built in nearly every scene—his own unnamed presence.

Dreiser's identification with his characters produces the composite personalities of Carrie/Dreiser, or Drouet/Dreiser, or Hurstwood/Dreiser. The ultimate effect becomes in *Sister Carrie* the expression of the powerful, omniscient presence of Dreiser, an integral part of every action, every attitude, every implicit and every expressed value.

As the passage continues, it is this personality that emerges rather than Carrie's:

> If she could but stroll up yon broad walk, cross that rich entrance-way, which to her was of the beauty of a jewel, and sweep in grace and luxury to possession and command—oh! how quickly would sadness flee; how in an instant, would the heartache end. She gazed and gazed, wondering, delighting, longing and all the while the siren voice of the unrestful was whispering in her ear.
>
> "If we could have such a home as that," said Mrs. Hale sadly, "how delightful it would be."
>
> "And yet they do say," said Carrie, "that no one is ever happy."

As an expression of Carrie's naive delight, wistful longing, and reflective philosophizing, the passage is somewhat unconvincing. But as an expression of the unseen presence of the author, who, through the technique of speaking through his characters, has entered the action of the novel, the passage is both believable and functional. Carrie here is something more than the simple girl drifting from one desire to another, one circumstance to the next. And it is that *something more* in Carrie that we respond to.

Why this unseen, unnamed presence should hold the key to the effective artistic meaning of the novel is the great challenge for Dreiser criticism. Certainly it is not in his simple, even sophomoric philosophy, not in those passages from which can be abstracted statements which relate Dreiser to philosophical naturalism. Rather, I believe, the literary power lies in the singular way Dreiser's sensibility, as that sensibility inheres in every scene, acts to become an expressive symbol for artistic meaning. What is meant by Dreiser's sensibility are his felt, rather than formulated, values—those values which produce his own special responsiveness to the pathetic in life, his special kind of caring for mankind, his honest, however naïve, probing into the mysteries of human motivation, his acute awareness of social cruelty, his sometimes reverential, sometimes bewildered, re-action to the way of life in America. It is this integra-tion of self and art that produces the voice of Dreiser.

And what we have continued to respond to in that voice is its authenticity as an expressive symbol. We are accustomed to think of expressive symbols as charac-teristic of the poem rather than the novel. Indeed, most attempts at applying critical techniques for examining poetry to works of fiction have been somewhat unre-warding. One feels, however, that the principle behind such attempts is sound—the principle, that is, which in-sists that the meaning in literary art resides in the special symbolic formulation of experience which the work represents. But it is possible that the dominant symbolic forms of the poem, the image of Prufrock, the patterns of metaphor in *The Waste Land,* the irony of *The Canonization,* are not the forms to be looked for in examining a work of fiction. The novel is not so economic, not so precise and clear-cut in the way its meanings are formulated. As F. R. Leavis reminds us, "Prose depends ordinarily on cumulative effect." What makes a work of fiction symbolically expressive must be sought with the same principle in mind which one had in approaching the poem—but without the preconceptions of poetry criticism.

In the total image of the old man in Eliot's poem *Gerontion* we have an effective expressive symbol of lost human purpose, of spiritual sterility. When the old man declares "The woman keeps the kitchen, makes tea,/ Sneezes at evening, poking the peevish gutter," we recognize and respond to the meaning which has been objectified in the image. There is, I believe, the same expressive power in the image of Carrie, standing anxious and uncertain before a Chicago shoe factory. But here the writer's sensibility is part of the effective power of the image.

> The entire metropolitan centre possessed a high and mighty air calculated to overawe and abash the common applicant, and to make the gulf between poverty and success seem both wide and deep.
>
> Into this important commercial region the timid Carrie went. She walked east along Van Buren Street through a region of lessening importance, until it deteriorated into a mass of shanties and coal-yards, and finally verged upon the river. She walked bravely forward, led by an honest desire to find employment and delayed at every step by the interest of the unfolding scene, and a sense of helplessness amid so much evidence of power and force which she did not understand. These vast buildings, what were they? These strange energies and huge interests, for what purpose were they there?

And then presently:

> It was wonderful, all vast, all far removed, and she sank in spirit inwardly and fluttered feebly at the

heart as she thought of entering any one of these mighty concerns and asking for something to do—something that she could do—anything.

It would be a mistake to dismiss the passage with the observation that Dreiser, unlike Eliot, has failed to create an objective image that could stand alone in evoking its meaning, that Dreiser has obtruded himself into what could have been a clear-cut depiction. Actually, without Dreiser's felt presence, the scene would be little more than a parody. Taken by itself the subject matter, a small-town girl seeking her first job in the big city, has all the triteness of a Horatio Alger situation. Yet I believe that informed with Dreiser's sensibility, a sensibility which incorporates and transforms a diction that would otherwise be verbose and naive, the passage is a successful instance of Dreiser's expressive power. Without the peculiar quality of meaning which results from viewing the American scene with a naive wonder at its magnificence and at the same time with a disappointment at its unconcerned indifference to the lot of a helpless individual—without that special quality of meaning, we would not have Dreiser.

It is not enough, however, to point to Dreiser's presence as an effective device for achieving expressive meaning; how that presence functions in the development of character and theme is also a necessary condition for understanding the power of the novel. Dreiser's concept of man as that concept determines the values of each of his three major characters is singularly consistent throughout the work. For Carrie, Drouet, and Hurstwood, the dominant consideration in life is materialistic success and its accompanying rewards. What one could become in a world dominated by men of wealth and power—by men schooled and skilled as opportunists—what one could become in such a world directed the plans, hopes, and actions of each of the novel's central figures. The ideal life for Carrie, Drouet, and Hurstwood was completely the same: the world of better living. The images of this world are put forth in nearly every scene of the novel, for they were the images which directed, consciously and unconsciously, man as Dreiser knew him to be. For Carrie, leaving Columbus City for Chicago, there was "the gleam of a thousand lights," "a blare of sound, a roar of life, a vast array of human lives."

Once in Chicago Carrie's vision of the better life did not extend to the standards of wealth, fashion, and success which later she grew to adopt. What she longed for was that state of material being which was just out of reach, but which she could reasonably aspire to. Her immediate focus is on the "shop girls":

> They were pretty in the main, some even handsome, with an air of independence and indifference which added, in the case of the more favoured, a certain piquancy. Their clothes were neat, in many instances fine, and wherever she encountered the eye of one it was only to recognize in it a keen analysis of her own position—her individual shortcomings of dress and that shadow of *manner* which she thought must hang about her and make clear to all who and what she was. A flame of envy lighted in her heart. She realized in a dim way how much the city held— wealth, fashion, ease—every adornment for women, and she longed for dress and beauty with a whole heart.

Again, when Carrie became established in the more favorable surroundings of Drouet's modest but comfortable apartment, Dreiser's more than sympathetic depiction of Carrie's values contributes to the special quality

of meaning which his way of viewing his characters
develops.

> Carrie was an apt student of fortune's ways—of for-
> tune's superficialities. Seeing a thing, she would im-
> mediately set to inquiring how she would look,
> properly related to it. Be it known that this is not fine
> feeling, it is not wisdom. The greatest minds are not
> so afflicted; and, on the contrary, the lower order of
> mind is not so disturbed. Fine clothes to her were a
> vast persuasion; they spoke tenderly and Jesuitically
> for themselves. When she came within earshot of
> their pleading, desire in her bent a willing ear.

The same guiding principle, the achievement of a better material life, conditioned Carrie's response to all people she encountered, whether they were merely passersby
or individuals with whom she was to develop an intimate
relationship. When the salesman who had succeeded in
engaging her in conversation on the train described Chicago to her, Dreiser enters Carrie's viewpoint to comment:

> There was a little ache in her fancy of all he described.
> Her insignificance in the presence of so much magnif-
> icence faintly afflicted her. She realized that hers was
> not to be a round of pleasure, and yet there was some-
> thing promising in all the material prospect he set
> forth.

For Dreiser she was "a half-equipped little knight, ven-
turing to reconnoitre the mysterious city and dreaming
wild dreams of some vague, far-off supremacy, which
should make it prey and subject."

But the actual scene, when Carrie arrived at her destination, was in direct contrast to her daydreams. Into
her fanciful imaginings, directly occasioned by the excitement and novelty of the train's approach to the big

city, Dreiser interposes the unpleasant actuality of the real situation:

A lean-faced, rather commonplace woman recognized Carrie on the platform and hurried forward.

"Why Sister Carrie!" she began, and there was a perfunctory embrace of welcome.

Carrie realized the change of affectional atmosphere at once. Amid all the image, uproar, and novelty she felt cold reality taking her by the hand. No world of light and merriment. No round of amusement. Her sister carried with her most of the grimness of shift and toil.

Here, in this simple beginning, is the pattern Dreiser is to follow throughout the lengthy and labored development of the work—a pattern which gains in expressive power through the varied presentation of its underlying theme: man is caught in the paradox of his own idealized image of the world and the dismal realistic actuality he inevitably encounters. Instead of the exciting freedom which she anticipated Carrie found herself imprisoned in the drab world of her sister's family. Her residence became a dismal third-floor apartment above a grocery store. Dreiser methodically describes the scene and at the same time reflects Carrie's response to it:

She felt the drag of a lean and narrow life. The walls of the room were discordantly papered. The floors were covered with matting and the hall laid with a thin rag carpet. One could see that the furniture was of that poor, hurriedly patched together quality sold by the installment houses.

Perhaps the most singular effect resulting from Dreiser's continual imposition of his own presence throughout the work is achieved by his sympathetic identification with each of his characters. Each of the three major figures in some way violates society's moral code—Carrie, by consenting to become Drouet's mistress and by allowing herself to be carried off by a man with wife and family; Drouet by enticing an innocent, nearly destitute girl to become his mistress; and Hurstwood by abandoning his home for another woman after stealing from his employer's safe. But in each case Dreiser's full labors are directed at justifying their actions. Carrie is painstakingly shown as having none of the characteristics of a fallen woman, no desires that were not wholly natural and understandable. Her consent to Drouet was scarcely her own decision; it was the decision of circumstance brought about by an innate desire for a better life in a world which offered no opportunity for betterment but the one at hand.

Dreiser presents her as simply accepting the help of an amiable, good-natured fellow at a time when refusal meant defeat. Drouet, on the other hand, is presented as equally justified. It was in his nature, Dreiser explains, to be drawn to attractive women. Yet the married state would have hindered, if not prevented, his achieving his image of the good life, that of a sophisticated man-about-town. Drouet felt sorry for Carrie, Dreiser tells us, when he encountered her on a downtown Chicago street, helpless, hungry, and shabbily dressed.

But it is Hurstwood who needs and receives the author's fullest attention. To justify Hurstwood's desire to abandon his family in favor of his friend's mistress, whom he misleads about his own married state, is perhaps Dreiser's greatest problem—but one which produces his greatest success at character presentation. Dreiser shows the unsatisfactory home life which Hurstwood must endure—a domestic situation in which a selfish, unpleasant wife struggles to improve her social position by bringing off a socially favorable marriage for her daughter. We are shown that for a man of middle age who has achieved a measure of success and position, the possibility of an intimate relationship with a young attractive girl was not only flattering but, in the light of his unsatisfactory relationship with his wife, quite probable. Obsessed by his infatuation for the girl and plagued by his growing aversion to his nagging wife, Hurstwood is driven to his inevitable act—making off with money and girl.

Viewed in abstraction from its carefully detailed context, such justifications are scarcely convincing. Yet informed by Dreiser's ever-present sensibility in complete identification with his central character, Hurstwood's situation becomes authentic and believable.

In the scene in which Hurstwood is pushed into the snow by the stage-door attendant we have a typical example. There is the obvious attempt at reportorial detachment. But as everywhere in Dreiser, the objective reporter gives way to the responsive observer.

He started around to the side door. Then he forgot what he was going for and paused, pushing his hands deeper to warm the wrists. Suddenly it returned. The stage door! That was it.

He approached the entrance and went in.

"Well?" said the attendant, staring at him. Seeing him pause, he went over and shoved him. "Get out of here," he said.

"I want to see Miss Madenda," he tried to explain, even as he was being hustled away. "I'm all right. I—"

The man gave him a last push and closed the door. As he did so Hurstwood slipped and fell in the snow. It hurt him, and some vague sense of shame returned. He began to cry and swear foolishly.

"God damned dog!" he said. "Damned old cur," wiping the slush from his worthless coat. "I—I hired such people as you once."

Now a fierce feeling against Carrie welled up—just

one fierce, angry thought before the whole thing slipped out of his mind.

Dreiser writes with the unhappy realization that mankind is caught in a mechanistic existence where even one's hopes and desires are determined by environment and happenstance. But he writes also with the unwavering conviction that humanity is a possible achievement —that sympathetic understanding of one's fellowman is at least one discernible value, if indeed it is the only value. It is this conviction which finds voice in Dreiser's style, in that powerful unnamed presence which gives his novels their unique expressive power.

4

Faulkner's *As I Lay Dying*

It is not surprising that when *As I Lay Dying* appeared in 1930 it was regarded as a somewhat impure brand of naturalism. The subject matter was characteristically sociological. It described a family of southern poor whites confronted with incredible hardships, including flood, fire, and biological mishap, making a journey to the family burial ground. It presented such shocking and bizarre aspects of the journey as the persistent and offensive odor of the decaying body, the circling buzzards that followed the wagon containing the homemade coffin, and the grotesque image of the holes bored through the coffin into the dead woman's face by a crazed child. The significance of the novel was seen to lie in the indomitable spirit and solidarity of the family, who doggedly surmounted the incredible obstacles of the journey in their determination to carry out a promise to the dead mother that her remains be placed in the burial ground of her father's family.

Seldom was such criticism concerned with matters of form and technique. The attitude seemed to be that Faulkner had chosen to use a stream-of-consciousness method in telling his story, and although his method complicated critical examination, the events and their interpretation could yet be gleaned from the work, in spite of the added complication of a complex technique. As an account of a somewhat pathetic family of southern poor whites compelled to undertake a journey beset with hardships, the novel did not attain the stature of a *Grapes of Wrath*, but the subject matter and theme were felt by the critics to belong to the same tradition.

But Faulkner's fiction is much more complex than Steinbeck's, much more experimental. From *Sartoris* to *Sanctuary* and from *Absalom, Absalom!* to *The Town*, Faulkner continually sought new forms through which he could give a fresher, more vivid presentation to his insights into human experience. His search for new fictional techniques testifies to his belief in the efficacy of fiction in capturing and communicating aspects of man's real experience that can be formulated in no other way. His experiment in *As I Lay Dying* is just such an achievement of meaning through form.

But experiment with form and technique necessarily implies deviation from the expected pattern, and, if the deviation is excessive, the work is often complex, even obscure. The charge of complexity and obscurity is a familiar one against modern artists, especially Joyce and Faulkner. The case of *As I Lay Dying* is typical. The division of the novel into short sections resembles the division into chapters of the more traditional form. But, since the actual unfolding of events fails to proceed as the reader of novels has been conditioned to expect, the pattern in Faulkner's novel may be difficult to discern.

Traditionally fiction means the narration of events, the unfolding of a story in time. Indeed, we have come to accept this characteristic as a necessary condition for fiction, even as its differentia as an art form. Yet what the artist does with this normative requirement has direct bearing on both his individual style and the significance of what he is able to formulate in and through that style. Both the story of what happened to the Joad family and the story of what happened to the Bundren family satisfy one fictional norm of time. In both, the story opens with something about to happen and proceeds with the unfolding of events until that something has happened. But Faulkner has made his fictional technique much more than the depiction of events. He has produced a symbolic form capable of expressing a deeper dimension of what it means to live in time.

In *As I Lay Dying* the time of human consciousness is not merely the time of the chronology of events. There is also a time of inner awareness which is an equally real aspect of human experience. For Faulkner, the time of inner awareness measures the intensity of human experience, not its order of succession.

It is when the reader recognizes that Faulkner is working with both kinds of time in *As I Lay Dying* that his experiment loses much of its obscurity. The complexity indeed remains, but it is a complexity charged with meaning. For what is also recognized is the twofold nature of human consciousness, the recognition that we live simultaneously in the world of external happenings as well as in the world of inner awarenesses, and that the order of events in the one is fundamentally different from the order of events in the other. Faulkner's task has been the simultaneous presentation of both; here is his subject matter for the novel.

By moving from the consciousness of one character to that of another in a continual shifting of viewpoint, Faulkner is able to present not only the pattern of events but also the pattern of individual existences with their attendant interpretations of event and motive. Thus the Darl of event is not the Darl of consciousness, for the former is presented primarily through the eyes of others. Similarly with each of the other characters—their existence as participants in a journey is generically different from their existence as living, experiencing beings, and it is through Faulkner's successful experiment that we are able to experience the ironic quality of the difference. Hence, for Faulkner the plot of human existence is double in nature, and in *As I Lay Dying* he has offered a fictional form which testifies to his conviction.

To the extent that we can view Darl objectively—as one who is different from the others, as one slightly peculiar at times, at times quite insane—to the extent such a view is possible, we are aware of Darl as a case history. But the objective view of Darl is not our only account. What Darl is essentially, what he is in his inner experiencing, pervades the entire book. Nearly one-third of the sixty-odd sections are devoted to presenting the inner Darl.

Faulkner is nowhere more successful than in depicting this complex individual. The reader's comprehension moves from the Darl of action and event to the Darl of inner consciousness. The paradoxical quality of the real Darl resides finally in the tension between these two different aspects of human experience. The Darl who taunts his brother with the fact of their mother's death because to his brother Addie's dying is too painful to face, the Darl who sees his sister's dilemma but offers only silent repudiation, the Darl who sets fire to the stock-filled barn of a helpful farmer in order to cremate his mother—such a Darl is easy to judge. He is accordingly jealous and vindictive, coldly lacking in family responsibility, and socially incompetent in his felonious act.

But the Darl of being, the Darl we know by Faulkner's discovery of a way "to see into the heart," is not easy to judge. Indeed, we are not moved to seek judgment. It is enough that we understand. Darl's doing, his external acts, the part he plays in the unfolding of events, become understandable in the light of our insight into the reality of his felt experience.

Faulkner's successful portrayal of such a character as

Darl changes our most fundamental questions about character and characterization. We are no longer so concerned with the unfolding of events, with the question "Then what happened?" as we are with the presentation of being, with the question "What is man's real experience?" Between Anse's simple question, "Where's Jewel?" and Darl's answer, "Down to the barn," we are made to experience something of the quality of Darl's living awareness.

> When I was a boy I first learned how much better water tastes when it has set awhile in a cedar bucket. Warmish-cool, with a faint taste like the hot July wind in cedar trees smells. It has to set at least six hours, and be drunk from a gourd. Water should never be drunk from metal.
>
> And at night it is better still. I used to lie on the pallet in the hall, waiting until I could hear them all asleep, so I could get up and go back to the bucket. It would be black, the shelf black, the still surface of the water a round orifice in nothingness, where before I stirred it awake with the dipper I could see maybe a star or two in the bucket, and maybe in the dipper a star or two before I drank.

Faulkner's writing here is exceptionally vivid; his images are lucid and flawless. But the real function of the imagery is not to describe a Mississippi boy's pleasant experience of drinking cool water on a hot summer night. Rather the passage functions to objectify the quality of the boy's sensibility. That is, we are not so much concerned with the nature of this particular experience as we are with the nature of the consciousness which was capable of such an experience.

The consciousness marking the greatest contrast with Darl's is that of Cora Tull. The contrast gives an impact to our sensibilities. Our interest is not with Cora's chick-

ens and eggs or with her baking cakes to sell to wealthy
ladies; rather we are interested in what these things are
as they objectify her preoccupations, as they reveal to us
the quality of her conscious experience, and as they express Cora's world, her values, and her relationship to
the action of the novel. It is what Cora essentially *is* as
that *is-ness* comes into immediate relation to
the Bundren family that gives rise to Jewel's explosive
utterance in the only section in which he is the viewpoint figure, and to Vardaman's disgust when he
throws in the dust the fish which he was proudly carrying to his mother.

Cora is important. Her facile moral pronouncements
become the ironic expression of some of the central
meanings of the novel. In an early section she declares:
"The Lord can see into the heart. If it is his will that
some folks has different ideas of honesty from other
folks, it is not my place to question his decree." Many
ironic ambiguities are present here. It is immediately apparent that Cora is blinded by her moral preconceptions from ever seeing into the heart of any human being
—especially herself. Further, the passage is related to
Faulkner's technique and the meaning which he is able
to formulate through that technique. Cora's utterance
is at once an objective symbol of her values and ironically enables the reader to "see into the heart."

Ultimately, the passage is related to the total meaning
of the work: the sympathetic depiction, devoid of moral
preconceptions, of living, experiencing mankind. For it
is Faulkner's chief task to present what he has found
man's nature to be—to present the "different ideas of
honesty" which define the human situation. And his
presentation is necessarily varied and complex—from
the spiritually blind Cora Tull to the supersensitively
aware Darl—a range that encompasses a world of humanity in its scope and requires a boldness of fictional

technique characteristic of the most successful experiments of modern fiction.

The scene in which Cora visits Addie just prior to Addie's dying is characteristic of Faulkner's technique and intention. Cora is present at Addie's bedside as a spectator whose interest is founded more on curiosity than on sympathy. The face she presents to the ladies of the sickroom is conventional enough. She believes she is doing her duty as friend and comforter. But in objectifying her inner awareness, Faulkner presents a much more real face of Cora Tull. Here is her consciousness reporting:

> The quilt is drawn up to her chin, hot as it is, with only her two hands and her face outside. She is propped on the pillow, with her head raised so she can see out the window, and we can hear him every time he takes up the adze or the saw. If we were deaf we could almost watch her face and hear him, see him.

Here is the Cora who has come to witness the approaching death of another human, to watch and note the face of the dying woman as she hears her coffin being built. Faulkner finds effective symbolic correlatives for her real feelings in concise successive images. We do not see Addie in them; we see Addie as Cora sees her; we see one aspect of Cora's essential self: "Her face is wasted away so that the bones draw just under the skin in white lines. Her eyes are like two candles when you watch them gutter down into the sockets of iron candlesticks." Then in one unexpected stroke, Faulkner gives us a deeper insight into Cora's being as she pronounces judgment: "But the eternal and everlasting salvation and grace is not upon her." And we see that for Cora, Addie is not Addie; she is the violation of Cora's understanding of a moral principle. Cora has labeled the picture she comes each day to witness, and what is

Addie has long since dissolved into Cora's label. Here is justification for Jewel's cry.

Like the buzzards that will circle the coffin throughout its long journey, the ladies of the sickroom are at once a presence that is both ludicrous and ominous—comic in what they suggest of gossipy, dissembling women, but tragically ominous in what they suggest of man's relationship to his fellowman. The unique quality of Faulkner's meaning resides neither in what Cora voices nor in what she thinks but in the tension between the two:

> "They turned out real nice," I say. "But not like the cakes Addie used to bake." You can see that girl's washing and ironing in the pillow slip, if ironed it ever was. Maybe it will reveal her blindness to her, laying there at the mercy and ministration of four men and a tomboy girl.

Cora, Kate, and Eula are an essential part of the scene as Addie Bundren lies dying. Cora's mind wanders from the real image of Addie: "Under the quilt she makes no more of a hump than a rail would, and the only way you can tell she is breathing is by the sound of the mattress shucks." Then her concern becomes the appropriateness of Eula's necklace which cost only twenty-five cents—abruptly she reflects on her own loss of the money for the cakes and finally on Eula's real reason for being present, the attention of Darl. In carrying out the deathbed ritual the ladies are fulfilling the requirement of their unquestioned mores. But in revealing the nature of their real feelings by objectifying those feelings in their sometimes trivial, sometimes vindictive preoccupations, Faulkner has created a larger symbol, one which suggests his artistic judgment of one aspect of man's essential nature. They are as blameless for their activity as are the buzzards but in the real quality of their consciousnesses, no less repulsive.

The fact of Darl's insanity raises the question of just how valid his insights are intended by Faulkner to be. And it is not merely a matter of the insanity occurring at the end of the journey. Anse, in his opening section, makes an indirect allusion to it:

> And Darl, too. Talking me out of him, durn them. It ain't that I am afraid of work; I always have fed me and mine and kept a roof above us: it's that they would shorthand me just because he tends to his own business, just because he's got his eyes full of the land, because the land laid up-and-down ways then; it wasn't till that ere road come and switched the land around longways and his eyes still full of the land, that they begun to threaten me out of him, trying to shorthand me with the law.

And so it is established early in the novel that Darl's sanity is suspect, even, it is suggested, to the point where incarceration is considered. Ironically it is Anse's selfish concern with being shorthanded that keeps Darl out of the asylum from the outset.

Yet Darl's insights and inner experiences are never presented as mere fantasy, never suggestive of Walter Mitty-like situations. They seem to be offered not only as adequate expressions of what is happening but also as symbolic expressions of Darl's incredible sensitivity. The section dealing with the death of Addie is perhaps the most successful instance of the technique. In the preceding section Peabody, the doctor, has been dismissed from the sickroom by the silent repudiation of the dying woman. In the final lines of his section he reports:

> Beyond the porch Cash's saw snores steadily into the board. A minute later she calls his name, her voice harsh and strong,
>   "Cash," she says; "you, Cash!"

Then in the next section, which is Darl's, is presented a detailed account of Addie's death. But it is Darl's imagined account, his experienced vision of the scene, which is presented. Darl and Jewel are miles away at the time, Darl having succeeded in keeping Jewel and Addie apart at the time of her death by urging the need for the three dollars which could be earned by hauling a wagonload of lumber. Anse, always greedy for another dollar, was an easy prey to Darl's intention. Jewel, refusing to admit that his mother's death was imminent and unable to face the possibility of it, had also consented to Darl's suggestion. Three short passages of the section are in italics. These passages function to locate Darl's actual position, far removed from the room in which Addie lies dying. The first begins:

> *Jewel, I say. Overhead the day drives level and grey, hiding the sun by a flight of grey spears. In the rain the mules smoke a little, splashed yellow with mud, the off one clinging in sliding lunges to the side of the road above the ditch. The tilted lumber gleams dull yellow, water-soaked and heavy as lead, tilted at a steep angle into the ditch above the broken wheel; about the shattered spokes and about Jewel's ankles a runnel of yellow neither water nor earth swirls.*

It is at this moment, having succeeded not only in separating Jewel from Addie but in rendering him completely impotent of action, that Darl's acutely authentic vision of Addie's death occurs. Here is the scene as Faulkner symbolizes its existence in the mind of Darl:

> Pa   stands   beside   the   bed.   From   behind   his leg Vardaman peers, with his round head and his eyes round and his mouth beginning to open. She looks at pa; all her failing life appears to drain into her eyes, urgent, irremediable. "It's Jewel she wants," Dewey Dell says.

"Why Addie," pa says, "him and Darl went to make one more load. They thought there was time. That you would wait for them, and that three dollars and all. . ."

He stoops, laying his hand on hers. For a while yet she looks at him, without reproach, without anything at all, as if her eyes alone are listening to the irrevocable cessation of his voice. Then she raises herself, who has not moved in ten days. Dewey Dell leans down, trying to press her back.

"Ma," she says; "ma."

She is looking out the window, at Cash stooping steadily at the board in the failing light, laboring on toward darkness and into it as though the stroking of the saw illumined its own motion; board and saw engendered.

"You, Cash," she shouts, her voice harsh, strong, and unimpaired. "You, Cash!"

Here is ample justification for accepting Darl's subjective experience as a valid account of what actually occurred. For Darl's report of Addie's last utterance is the same as Peabody's. The fact makes credible Darl's amazing insight and lends authenticity to his judgments.

Darl's sensibility is most acute when it is focused on Jewel. Every nuance of Jewel's discernible emotion and action registers upon Darl's awareness. When Anse's question, "Where's Jewel?" calls Darl's attention to Jewel's presence in the barn, Darl pictures his brother: "Down there fooling with that horse. He will go on through the barn into the pasture. The horse will not be in sight." Then abruptly Faulkner changes from the future tense reflecting Darl's imagined view of the scene to the present tense—as if Darl were actually reporting the scene. Again what is most important is not the event itself but the actuality which Darl experiences in it.

He [the horse] is up there among the pine seedlings, in the cool. Jewel whistles, once and shrill. The horse snorts, then Jewel sees him, glinting for a gaudy instant among the blue shadows.

The meaning which Faulkner is able to achieve through this technique is amazingly complex. Darl suddenly becomes the author of Jewel's experience. We accept the viewpoint as Jewel's, that the horse for Jewel is "glinting for a gaudy instant among the blue shadows." Yet we are aware that the whole depiction is a projection of Darl's imagined account. The meaning which emerges is that Darl's acute sensitivity has invaded the awareness of his brother, that not only is Darl constantly aware of his brother's external actions but he is also profoundly aware, in his valid imaginings, of Jewel's inner experience.

The reason for Darl's obsession with his brother is not presented for some hundred pages, but until the reader becomes cognizant of it, Darl remains an inexplicable figure. When Jewel was fifteen, Darl, then slightly older, came to the realization of Addie's infidelity—and to the realization of her love for Jewel. Here was the experience that conditioned what he was during the time of the story, the time of Addie's death and the journey. All of his feelings have become centered by now on his deep resentment of Jewel—the objectification of his grief and incompleteness.

In a story by D. H. Lawrence, "The Rocking Horse Winner," the deep, primal need of a boy for the love of his mother, a need which because of her very nature she is incapable of satisfying, expresses itself in violent and desperate action to remove the obstacle between himself and his mother: her obsessive craving for money. Lawrence's story suggests the dormant, slumbering forces in man's nature—forces which come into being when psychological development is threatened by the nonful-fillment of a vital need. Love, too, becomes a force, measurable only because of its absence. The effect on Lawrence's boy and the effect on Darl show remarkable similarities: both withdraw into a lonely isolation and introspection; both develop a heightened sensitivity and awareness; in both appears an obsessive preoccupation with the obstacle that blocks their completeness. For the boy the embodiment of the obstacle is money; for Darl it is Jewel, the living symbol of his frustration.

Nearly every one of Darl's nineteen viewpoint sections is in some way an expression of Darl's obsessive preoccupation with his brother. Eleven open with this preoccupation, and five others are centrally concerned with it. Some examples of these openings reveal the way Faulkner builds this important expressive symbol of Darl's inner world. The book begins with a Darl section: "Jewel and I come up from the field, following the path in a single file." Darl's third section opens: "We watch him come around the corner and mount the steps. He does not look at us. 'You ready?' he says." And his fourth section: "He has been to town this week: the back of his neck is trimmed close, with a white line between hair and sunburn like a joint of white bone. He has not once looked back."

As Darl and Jewel return to the family who have been waiting to begin the long journey to the cemetery in Jefferson, Darl's obsessive hatred for his brother emerges in the first expression of the bitter taunts he is to voice throughout the journey. The section opens: " 'It's not your horse that's dead, Jewel,' I say." The expression picks up the earlier phrase, "Jewel, I say," which had not been voiced but had been significantly a part of Darl's conscious thought. Darl's taunts continue as he points to the buzzards circling the house containing the body of the dead Addie. He has succeeded, not only in keeping

Jewel from the side of his dying mother, but in delaying
for two additional days the departure for the cemetery.
The buzzards are an added affront to the pride and dignity of Jewel who had, in his only viewpoint section,
lashed out at the indignities attending the dying of
Addie: Cash's construction of the coffin in Addie's presence, the neighboring women "sitting like buzzards in
the sick room," and Dewey Dell's "keeping the air always moving so fast on her face that when you're tired
you can't breathe it." It is these violations of pride and
dignity that give rise to his tragic outburst and reveal the
depth of his feeling for his mother:

> It would just be me and her on a high hill and me
> rolling the rocks down the hill at their faces, picking
> them up and throwing them down the hill, faces and
> teeth and all by God until she was quiet and not that
> goddam adze going one lick less. One lick less and we
> could be quiet.

Darl, fully aware of his brother's values, is thus moved
to use those values to increase the intensity and incisive-
ness of his taunts: " 'See them?' I say. High above the
house, against the quick thick sky, they hang in narrow-
ing circles. From here they are no more than specks,
implacable, patient, portentous." Then, aware that
Jewel, through prolonged effort, had succeeded in estab-
lishing the horse as a surrogate for his mother, as a way
of release from the overwhelming intensity of their relationship, Darl probes the psychological wound in Jewel's
personality: " 'But it's not your horse that's dead.' 'Goddamn you,' he says. 'Goddamn you.' " Immediately
juxtaposed is Darl's pathetic motive: "I cannot love my
mother because I have no mother."

To understand Darl's isolation and loneliness, his sensitivity and his obsession with his brother, it is necessary
to examine his relationship with Addie, the one who

determined the direction his psychological development would take. The single viewpoint section presented through the consciousness of Addie has no location within the unfolding events of the story. It is the voice of one giving an account of her life, a voice explaining and justifying her action in an existence in which she is no longer involved in action. The section opens with a reminiscence of her experiences with the children in her schoolroom just prior to her marriage to Anse.

> In the afternoon when school was out and the last one had left with his little dirty snuffling nose, instead of going home I would go down the hill to the spring where I could be quiet and hate them.

The passage resembles the beginning of a confession. In it the speaker faces the reality of her feelings toward the children directly. There is no circumlocution for the word "hate," because there is no recognition of the conventional preconceptions toward hating which one finds and expects in the values of Addie's moralistic neighbor, Cora Tull. Addie's values, integrally related to her attitude toward the children, are offered at once. We see that her hatred of the children is not for their runny noses or unfinished lessons, but for their individuation, their withdrawal into their secret selves, their native instinct to refuse communion with another by shutting that other out of their awarenesses. For Addie such individuation meant death in life.

> I could just remember how my father used to say that the reason for living was to get ready to stay dead a long time. And when I would have to look at them day after day, each with his and her secret and selfish thought, and blood strange to each other blood and strange to mine, and think that this seemed to be the only way I could get ready to stay dead, I would hate my father for having ever planted me.

In her marriage to Anse, Addie encountered the great disappointment of her life. Like the children's, Anse's world was completely self-centered, shared with no one and kept impregnable by the conventional abstractions and labels which could readily be attached to any act or intention. For Addie there was no marriage of real selves, no violation of her aloneness, no real communion with another.

> He [Anse] had a word, too. Love, he called it. But I had been used to words for a long time. I knew that that word was just like the others: just a shape to fill a lack.

Throughout Addie's long confession, we see the gradual development of an image of a woman of great physical and spiritual vitality, dedicated to a conviction that life must be shared to be meaningful, that withdrawal meant rejection of one's responsibility to live meaningfully, and that the reason for living was to get ready to stay dead a long time. Addie's bitter disappointment with her marriage to Anse reaches a climax after the unexpected and unwanted birth of Darl:

> He [Anse] did not know that he was dead, then. Sometimes I would lie by him in the dark, hearing the land that was of my blood and flesh, and I would think: Anse. Why Anse. Why are you Anse. I would think about his name until after a while I could see the word as a shape, a vessel, and I would watch him liquefy and flow into it like cold molasses flowing out of the darkness into the vessel, until the jar stood full and motionless: a significant shape profoundly without life like an empty door frame.

It was at this point that Addie abandoned her marriage to Anse. Though she continued to stay with the family, she no longer considered Anse and the children

who were to follow from their spiritually sterile relationship as her children. She had admitted her acceptance of
her firstborn, Cash:

> that when the right time came, you wouldn't need a
> word [love] for that any more than for pride or fear.
> Cash did not need to say it to me nor I to him.

But Darl was rejected:

> Then I found that I had Darl. At first I would not
> believe it. Then I believed that I would kill Anse. It
> was as though he had tricked me, hidden within a
> word like within a paper screen and struck me in the
> back through it.

The product of her relationship with Whitfield, the
minister, was Jewel, the object of her full acceptance
and love.

> And so I have cleaned my house. With Jewel—I lay
> by the lamp, holding up my own head watching him
> [the doctor] cap and suture it before he breathed—
> the wild blood boiled away and the sound of it ceased.

Addie's final pronouncement reveals the reason for Darl's
pathetic situation:

> I gave Anse Dewey Dell to negative Jewel. Then I
> gave him Vardaman to replace the child I had robbed
> him of. And now he has three children that are his
> and not mine. And then I could get ready to die.

The "three children that are his and not mine" are, of
course, Darl, Dewey Dell, and Vardaman.

Addie's revelation of her conviction that the purpose
in human existence is to be found in relationships that
are experienced rather than those which are distilled
through abstractions provides insight into her individual values and defines the ground of her moral action.

In the light of that conviction, we can understand not only her special "hate" for the schoolchildren but also the justification for her mildly violent relationship toward them.

> I would look forward to the times when they faulted, so I could whip them. When the switch fell I could feel it upon my flesh; when it welted and ridged it was my blood that ran, and I would think with each blow of the switch: Now you are aware of me! Now I am something in your secret and selfish life, who have marked your blood with my own forever and ever.

And presently:

> I knew that it had been, not that they had dirty noses, but that we had had to use one another by words like spiders dangling by their mouths from a beam, swinging and twisting and never touching, and that only through the blows of the switch could my blood and their blood flow as one stream.

It is with this account of her action that we can understand Darl's somewhat plaintive observation of Jewel's relationship with Addie: "Ma always whipped and petted him more." It accounts for Darl's insight into Jewel's semiviolent relationship with the horse, the violence recognizable as an essential part of the love between man and animal.

> He enters the stall and waits until it kicks at him so that he can slip past and mount on to the trough and pause, peering out across the intervening stalltops toward the empty path, before he reaches into the loft. "Goddamn him. Goddamn him."

For Darl there has been no such relationship with another and his cry of hatred is understandable more as an expression of his pathetic lot than as evidence of his vindictiveness.

Similarly, the promise which Addie elicited from Anse that she would be buried in Jefferson can be understood only after her values are understood. Her relationship to Anse is not the relationship of a loving wife to a devoted husband who has dedicated himself to the carrying out of her wishes—the meaning that a sociological criticism of the novel would suggest. Rather quite the opposite is true. The promise is Addie's revenge for the destruction of her life by the clash between her own and Anse's values. His shallow concept of love and her deep desire for an experienced love meant only frustration and unfulfillment for Addie.

> But then I realized that I had been tricked by words older than Anse or love, and that the same word had tricked Anse too, and that my revenge would be that he would never know I was taking revenge. And when Darl was born I asked Anse to promise to take me back to Jefferson when I died.

Here is the real motive for the promise, a motive that is rooted in Addie's values. She knows that Anse who lives by words will remain consistent with his ways. The irony is that those ways have been responsible not only for Addie's tragic situation but for the tragic lives of those children she has, because of her feelings toward her husband, repudiated.

Thus in *As I Lay Dying* Faulkner is not writing simply out of a belief that man will endure in the face of hardship. He is writing out of a conviction that what is most real in human experience is the kind of inner world man inhabits—a world wherein is determined man's feelings, hopes, desires, aspirations, compulsions, and obsessions, and ultimately his attitudes and actions in his relationships with his fellowman.

5

Hemingway's *The Old Man and the Sea*

In *The Old Man and the Sea*, Hemingway presents his most satisfactory resolution to the problem that he raises throughout his major works, the problem of man's individual values in a world that is either prudently materialistic or ultimately malevolent. When the problem of man is treated by the writers of the naturalist tradition, the presentation is inevitably uncomplex. For Dreiser, man is helplessly caught in a mechanistic universe. His problem is, at base, survival, his norm adjustment, and his goal materialistic success. Dreiser's task was to present one world, the only world he envisioned, a world external to the individual. His characters are objects placed within the myriad thrusts and drives which he found to be characteristic of that world. For the Dreiser hero, the problem of the being of the individual was no problem: the building of an individual integrity meant simply the development of one's capacity for making the most out of every opportunity.

But Hemingway is not a naturalistic writer; he presents two worlds. On the one hand he envisions an internal world of singularly human values where the chief concern is with the being of the individual. On the other he recognizes the external world of naturalistic values where the central focus is on the hopeless plight of man caught in the mechanism of a malevolent universe. Thus Hemingway's question is much more complex than

Dreiser's: What is to be the role of the individual man in a world which acts at every turn to determine his destiny? This is the basic problem throughout Hemingway's fiction. It is the problem confronting the young Hemingway hero Nick Adams in "The Killers." His answer is characteristic of a pattern Hemingway was to follow in nearly every work prior to *The Old Man and the Sea*: to detach himself from an environment whose value conditions he could not accept.

In another of the early stories, "Soldier's Home," Krebs, the young soldier who has just returned from the war, gives a similar answer, but here the justification for withdrawal is more fully developed. And it is that justification which must be examined, for it constitutes the major theme in all of Hemingway's works. Faced on all sides with an incessant pressure to conform to the compromise with values which Krebs believes most people in his town have made, he remains stoically resolute against those values. He refuses to become caught up in the social alliances of the young girls, the submission to just any job, the acceptance of the role of the aspiring young man. In the violence and chaos of war he had discovered the values of self-integrity, the importance of moral action which had come spontaneously and which produced his "feeling cool and clear inside," and he was determined to maintain that new sense of being which he had experienced.

In Hemingway's three major novels the central problem is basically the same. Jake Barnes of *The Sun Also Rises* had become an expatriate whose sense of morality, while unconventional, was the most important reality in his life. Similarly Frederick Henry of *A Farewell to Arms* had left to fight in the war of a foreign country. But again what was most real for him was his search for meaning—a search described by Robert Penn Warren as fundamentally religious. And Robert Jordan, the hero of

For Whom the Bell Tolls, also engaged in a cause not his own, discovers that keeping alive one's rightness of individual being is more important than keeping alive a social cause or even oneself.

But what is perhaps most significant in Hemingway's various treatments of the problem of individual values is the fact that maintaining one's integrity is not so much a choice as it is a necessity. In "The Snows of Kilimanjaro" he creates the pathetic image of a man who had compromised his sense of integrity. The story portrays the bitterness of a writer who was forced by his compromise to live a lie. Confronted with the fact of his rapidly approaching death, he remembers "all the things he had wanted to write about," and he realizes that it was precisely because his life had been a lie that he was now creatively impotent. In a passage depicting his self-reflection, we see the cause of his unhappy state.

> You kept from thinking and it was all marvelous. You were equipped with good insides so that you did not go to pieces that way, the way most of them had, and you made an attitude that you cared nothing for the work you used to do, now that you could no longer do it. But, in yourself, you said that you would write about these people; about the very rich; that you were really not one of them but a spy in their country; that you would leave it and write of it and for once it would be written by someone who knew what he was writing of. But he would never do it, because each day of not writing, of comfort, of being that which he despised, dulled his ability and softened his will to work so that, finally, he did no work at all.

Here is an important theme in Hemingway's fiction: the correspondence between one's work and one's existence. Whether a man is a writer, a bullfighter, a surgeon, or a fisherman, to "get it right" technically is not only as important as to "get it right" morally but completely dependent upon one's morality. Thus the real problem facing each of Hemingway's heroes is not merely to develop and maintain his skill in his work; rather it is to develop and maintain a clear sense of his essential self. Harry's confused image of himself is presented as the direct result "of being that which he despised." We discover that Harry's intention in withdrawing from the decadent life of the cosmopolitan set was to recover his sense of individual being.

> Africa was where he had been happiest in the good time of his life, so he had come out here to start again. They had made this safari with a minimum of comfort. There was no hardship; but there was no luxury and he had thought that he could get back into training that way. That in some way he could work the fat off his soul the way a fighter went into the mountains to work and train in order to burn it out of his body.

Thus the story of Harry is the story of a man who was cut off by an untimely death while he was attempting to regain his spiritual life. He is one of the few central characters in all of Hemingway's works who is presented as a pathetic figure, not so much because he is the unfortunate victim of chance circumstance—but because he is the unwitting victim, through weak moral choice, of his own lost values.

But in the portrayal of Santiago in *The Old Man and the Sea* there is no such uncertainty of being, no confusion of self and values. The old man is presented from beginning to end as one who has achieved true existence. His response to every situation is the response of a spiritually fulfilled man. The story, then, is not concerned with the familiar Hemingway search for values; rather it is concerned with the depiction of conflicting values.

Throughout five carefully delineated sections of the novel, the center of focus is always on the image of the old man. The first section concerns the old man and the boy; the second, the old man and the sea; the third, the old man and the marlin; the fourth, the old man and the sharks; the fifth section returns to the old man and the boy.

In the opening section Santiago is shown to be something of a pathetic figure. He is old, alone, except for the friendship of a young boy, and now even dependent to a degree upon the charity of others for his subsistence. His situation is symbolized by the condition of his sail which was "patched with flour sacks and, furled, it looked like the flag of permanent defeat." For eighty-four days he had fished without success and had lost his apprentice because the boy's parents had considered him *"salao,"* "the worst form of unlucky."

But almost at once the tone of the writing changes. Only in external appearances is the old man pathetic. Hemingway reverses the attitude toward the old man in a single stroke: "Everything about him was old except his eyes and they were the same color as the sea and were cheerful and undefeated." The contrast in meaning is evident: to be defeated in the business of fishing is not to be a defeated man. The theme begins and ends the novel; never, after the opening lines, does the reader regard Santiago as defeated. The point is made emphatic in the final conversation between the old man and the boy:

"They beat me, Manolin," he said. "They truly beat me."

"*He* didn't beat you. Not the fish."

And the old man, whose thoughts have been on a much more profound level of contesting, replies, " 'No. Truly. It was afterwards.' "

The novel's concern, then, is with success and failure; more precisely, with kinds of success and kinds of failure. The central contrast is between the two fundamental levels of achievement: practical success and success in the achievement of being. Similarly the novel posits two kinds of defeat: failure to compete successfully in a materialistic, opportunistic world where this only is the measure of a man, and failure to maintain one's being regardless of external defeat. Thus the real story concerns the meaning, in terms of fundamental human values, of human existence.

Almost at once we become aware that the misleading initial depiction of the old man as a somewhat pathetic figure is the direct result of viewing him only from the standpoint of his recent prolonged ill luck. Had Hemingway continued to present Santiago through the eyes that measure a man's worth merely in terms of his practical success or failure, the novel would necessarily have been a naturalistic one. Santiago's skill, determination, and nobility of spirit would simply have contributed to the greater irony of his finally catching a prize fish only to worsen his lot by losing it.

But the key to all of Hemingway's major characters is never to be found, as it is with Dreiser's characters, in merely what happens to them. Rather it is to be found in what they essentially are. This is not to discount the importance in Hemingway of environmental forces, both man-made and cosmic, acting to condition and even to determine human destiny. In fact, those whose values do not follow from the shaping forces of environment are few in number, rarely to be encountered. Santiago is one. And in his age and wisdom and simplicity he constantly reminds himself and the boy, who is learning from him, of the distinction. It is a subtle but vital distinction, one which Santiago never loses sight of. When the boy complains to Santiago about the attitude of his

new master, Santiago's response is central to the underlying theme of the novel. The boy points out:

> "He brings our gear himself. He never wants any-
> one to carry anything."
> "We're different," the old man said.

The real story of *The Old Man and the Sea* begins
with this distinction. In the first section two indistinct
characters are introduced who embody the values of the
practical world, the boy's father and the successful fisherman to whom the boy is assigned. In the old man's
and the boy's discussion of their enforced separation, we
see the old man's simple recognition of the problem.

> "Santiago," the boy said to him as they climbed
> the bank from where the skiff was hauled up. "I could
> go with you again. We've made some money."
> The old man had taught the boy to fish and the boy
> loved him.
> "No," the old man said. "You're with a lucky boat.
> Stay with them."
> "But remember how you went eighty-seven days
> without fish and then we caught big ones every day for
> three weeks."
> "I remember," the old man said. "I know you did
> not leave me because you doubted."
> "It was papa made me leave. I am a boy and I must
> obey him."
> "I know," the old man said. "It is quite normal."

But the old man's response means something more
than that it is quite normal for a boy to obey his parents; it means the acknowledgment that materialism is
the central criterion for action and values in the practical
world. And the passage also suggests that the boy has
been taught something more than how to fish; he has
been taught authentic love and respect, values which he

now finds conflicting with the practical demands of his parents.

The successful fisherman, the unnamed "he" who is the boy's new master, is, in spite of his success at catching fish, totally without respect in the boy's eyes. When Santiago promises to awaken the boy in time for his day's work with his new master, the boy declares: " 'I do not like for him to waken me. It is as though I were inferior.' " The missing quality in the boy's new relationship is evident: the old man wakens the boy in order to share living with him; the impersonal "him" wakes the boy in order to use him.

Both the old man and the boy are keenly aware of their loss of each other, and both plan ways to regain their former relationship. It is here that Santiago discloses his decision to go "far out."

> "Tomorrow is going to be a good day with the currents," he said.
>
> "Where are you going?" the boy asked.
>
> "Far out to come in when the wind shifts. I want to be out before it is light."
>
> "I'll try to get him to work far out," the boy said. "Then if you hook something truly big we can come to your aid."

The old man's decision to go "far out" is a conscious decision. It was made with a skilled fisherman's awareness of recognized limitations, not in an attempt to challenge those limitations or to discover new ones, but in an attempt to oppose the forces of ill luck and the realistic demands of a materialistic society. It is the same kind of response of being that required his dogged opposition to the sharks, a response directed not at changing or reforming evil but simply and necessarily at opposing it. Then once again the distinction between the values of the old man and the values of the practical fisherman is made.

For Santiago the term for the distinction is "strange," a term which grows in significance throughout the novel:

> "He does not like to work too far out."
> "No," the boy said. "But I will see something which he cannot see such as a bird working and get him to come out after dolphin."
> "Are his eyes that bad?"
> "He is almost blind."
> "It is strange," the old man said. "He never went turtle-ing. That is what kills the eyes."
> "But you went turtle-ing for years off the Mosquito Coast and your eyes are good."
> "I am a strange old man."

To be strange is to possess values that are "different," values which enable man to transcend what Hemingway elsewhere has called the "biological trap" of a naturalistic existence.

There is no condemnation by the old man of those who do not share his values. He simply thinks of them as lacking wisdom, of being young or inexperienced.

> Many of the fishermen made fun of the old man and he was not angry. Others, of the older fishermen, looked at him and were sad. But they did not show it and they spoke politely about the current and the depths they had drifted their lines at and the steady good weather and of what they had seen.

For the "older fishermen," the "those who belong" of the earlier novels, a man's worth is not dependent upon his practical success. Ill luck may contribute to or even bring about one's failure in the world of practical values, but it cannot change what he essentially is within himself. Thus, for the initiate, respect and recognition are not contingent upon chance; they are the acknowledgment of the achievement of being. And it is a central maxim in Hemingway's concept of man that one's inner being must be constant regardless of the chance happenings of an external world.

The novel's second section presents the full significance of what it means to possess the sense of true existence. Just as the "he" who wakes the boy to use him is blocked by his practical ends from the experience of love so also the "younger fishermen" whose intention is to exploit are prevented from regarding the sea as anything more than "a contestant or a place or even an enemy." Again the distinction is one of individual values.

> He always thought of the sea as *la mar* which is what people call her in Spanish when they love her. Sometimes those who love her say bad things of her but they are always said as though she were a woman. Some of the younger fishermen, those who used buoys as floats for their lines and had motorboats, bought when the shark livers had brought much money, spoke of her as *el mar* which is masculine. They spoke of her as a contestant or a place or even an enemy. But the old man always thought of her as feminine and as something that gave or withheld great favours, and if she did wild or wicked things it was because she could not help them. The moon affects her as it does a woman, he thought.

The passage is an important one in the development of the novel. Hemingway's theme is clear: Success in the achievement of being carries with it the most valued of man's possessions, the capacity for love. And Santiago's capacity is everywhere evident. Once far out in the Gulf, the old man takes his place as a true inhabitant of his true environment. He responds to the sea and the sky and the birds and the fish with the pure response of his achieved being:

> He loved green turtles and hawks-bills with their elegance and speed and their great value and he had a friendly contempt for the huge, stupid loggerheads, yellow in their armour-plating, strange in their love-making, and happily eating the Portuguese men-of-war with their eyes shut.

One is reminded of the philosopher's statement, "Being consents to being," as Santiago's being responds to the creatures about him.

> During the night two porpoises came around the boat and he could hear them rolling and blowing. He could tell the difference between the blowing noise the male made and the sighing blow of the female.
> "They are good," he said. "They play and make jokes and love one another. They are our brothers like the flying fish."

Nowhere in all of Hemingway's works can be found such a direct treatment of genuine sentiment. One is reminded of Pound's statement that the writer in our time must necessarily be ironic and indirect to be effective. But in the simple image of the old man's identification with the creatures of the sea we have a rare instance of positive values being directly and effectively presented. Yet perhaps it is because there is everywhere present the lurking dangers of the dark water and the old man's realistic awareness of those malevolent forces that his love emerges fully as realistic as the ever-present threats which surround him.

Santiago's struggle with the marlin is the principal subject of the long third section. From the moment he feels the fish touch the bait, his feeling is one of joy for the anticipated contest:

> Then he felt the gentle touch on the line and he was happy.

"It was only his turn," he said. "He'll take it."

He was happy feeling the gentle pulling and then he felt something hard and unbelievably heavy.

Throughout the long contest his attitude toward the fish remains constant:

"Fish," he said. "I love you and respect you very much. But I will kill you dead before this day ends."

Let us hope so, he thought.

The events of the struggle are dramatic: from the time the fish is hooked, about noon of the first day, until the fish is killed, about noon of the third day, the old man is forced to place his own body between the fish and the boat. Fastening the line to the boat would result in the breaking of the line by any sudden lurch or swift motion by the fish. Thus the contest means for Santiago the summoning of his greatest efforts in skill and endurance. He carefully plans his strategy: constant maximum pressure on the line must be maintained in order to wear down the resistance of the fish and to encourage him to surface in an attempt to dislodge the hook. Santiago knew that once having surfaced, the fish would be unable to dive deep again. Nourishment and rest must be systematically apportioned to his body so that he would not lose the battle prematurely through physical exhaustion. All effort must point to the final struggle which would involve not merely skill and physical endurance but will, his own will in mortal contest with the will of the marlin.

But the real power of the novel's impact does not lie merely in the events of the old man's dramatic struggle. It lies, I believe, in Hemingway's successful creation of a new dimension in dramatic portraiture. In each of the five carefully delineated sections of the novel, the reader's attention is always on Santiago. But in each, Hemingway alters with subtle but masterful strokes his changing image of the old man. In each he modifies the dramatic focus to isolate, intensify, and thereby magnify the novel's central and controlling image, the portrait of Santiago.

In the setting of the simple fishing village we are presented with the aged fisherman, initially pathetic in his meager existence, but admirable in his determination to break his run of bad luck, at once lovable in his touching relationship with a young boy and quaint in his concern for American baseball. But as a solitary figure on the sea, against a backdrop of cosmic nature, the image of the old man takes on new and greater proportions. He becomes a being among the beings of the sea, a human force among the forces of the natural world. But it is at the point at which the old man engages the great marlin that a more profound level of meaning is reached. Hemingway marks the shift with characteristic restraint. The change is simple but unmistakable: "The boat began to move slowly off toward the North-West."

It is here, I think, that the reader becomes aware that he is experiencing the achievement in prose which Hemingway had tried vaguely to explain in *Green Hills of Africa*. He had referred there to "a fourth and fifth dimension that can be gotten." And in speaking of the complexity of such writing, he had declared, "Too many factors must combine to make it possible." He had called such prose "much more difficult than poetry," but one that "can be written, without tricks and without cheating. With nothing that will go bad afterwards." In the amazing combination of simple realism of narrative and complex symbolism of image at once contained in *The Old Man and the Sea*, Hemingway has, I believe, constructed his closest approximation to his goal.

On the realistic level the fisherman has hooked a

huge fish, so powerful that it begins to pull the boat. But now the symbolic level becomes more fully engaged, operating not to weaken the dramatic quality of the action, but to complement and intensify it. As the boat moves off to the northwest the old man's last contact with the land, "the tops of the blue hills that showed white," at once was lost. The total isolation of the old man as he is being drawn by the fish into unknown regions of the sea provides the focus which Hemingway needs for the full functioning of his art. Almost immediately the tone takes on a Melvillian character, chiefly in the reflections of the old man: " 'I'm being towed by a fish and I'm the towing bitt.' " Just as Melville was able to turn the most superficial description of whaling lore to a profound formulation of metaphysical speculation, so also Hemingway moves from the simple responses and reflections of the old man as he battles the fish to an abrupt application to deeper meaning.

"I wish the boy was here," he said aloud and settled himself against the rounded planks of the bow and felt the strength of the great fish through the line he held across his shoulders moving steadily toward whatever he had chosen.

When once, through my treachery, it had been necessary to him to make a choice, the old man thought.

His choice had been to stay in the deep dark water far out beyond all snares and traps and treacheries. My choice was to go there to find him beyond all people. Beyond all people in the world. Now we are joined together and have been since noon. And no one to help either one of us.

It is clear that Hemingway's intention is much more complex than the mere reporting of a dramatic action.

The actual event, the instinctive movement of the hooked fish toward some region of its native habitat is understood. But this is hardly Hemingway's subject matter. Presented through the sensibility of the old man the realistic event becomes transformed into a new subject matter—one which maintains the realism of the action, but which uses that action to objectify essentially human values and human responses. Santiago, the fisherman, participates in action, the action required for his practical livelihood, but Santiago, the man, also participates in existence, and human existence as he has achieved it is not confined by the limitations of a naturalistic existence. The choice of the fish, however native to its instinct, had been to live beyond the snares and traps and treacheries of those who would destroy him. There is a note of compassion and regret in the old man's declaration: "My choice was to go there to find him beyond all people. Beyond all people in the world." The response is a contradiction to Santiago's earlier feeling of happiness, of "joy for the anticipated contest." Yet the very ambivalence expresses at once something of the paradox of the human situation.

Even the simple sentiments of love and benevolence which Santiago feels for the small creatures of the sea become more profoundly valid when they are presented through the larger awareness of the old man. He knows that the sea which he loves can also be cruel, and his ambivalent attitude toward the sea intensifies the presentation of the paradox.

He was very fond of flying fish as they were his principal friends on the ocean. He was sorry for the birds, especially the small delicate dark terns that were always flying and looking and almost never finding and he thought, "The birds have a harder life than we do except for the robber birds and the heavy strong ones. Why did they make birds so delicate and fine as

those sea swallows when the ocean can be so cruel?
She is kind and very beautiful. But she can be so
cruel and it comes so suddenly and such birds that
fly, dipping and hunting, with their small sad voices
are made too delicately for the sea."

The passage contains an implicit lament. The old man's
question is reminiscent of Ahab's unhappy speculation
on the forces of malice in the universe. Yet there is no
defiance or anger directed to the impersonal "they"
who have made a universe which permits the simultaneous existence of good and evil, of helplessness and
gentleness amid destructive forces. Rather in the old
man's reflections there is all the sympathy and compassion of an awareness capable of comprehending the
paradoxical mystery of the struggle for existence.

But mysticism and metaphysics, like the many refer-
ences to the ordeal and suffering of Christ, do not function to create an allegory. Rather they function as poetic
allusion, to suggest something of the fundamental
nature of the old man's encounter with the great
marlin and its subsequent loss to the malevolent sharks.
Hemingway never loses sight of the old man as a simple fisherman who leads a simple life with simple purposes. In spite of the numerous metaphysical reveries
concerning the nature of human and cosmic purpose,
we are continually brought back to the old man's
simple existence—by his practice of making light of his
profundities, by his good-natured poking of fun at himself and his speculations. Yet the suggestions of deeper
meaning have been made, and their effect has been felt
by the reader. The image of the old man is at once an
achieved integration of existential simplicity and complexity:

A small bird came toward the skiff from the north.
He was a warbler and flying very low over the water.
The old man could see that he was very tired.

The bird made the stern of the boat and rested there. Then he flew around the old man's head and rested on the line where he was more comfortable.

"How old are you?" the old man asked the bird. "Is this your first trip?"

The bird looked at him when he spoke. He was too tired even to examine the line and he teetered on it as his delicate feet gripped it fast.

"It's steady," the old man told him. "It's too steady. You shouldn't be that tired after a windless night. What are birds coming to?"

The hawks, he thought, that come out to sea to meet them. But he said nothing of this to the bird who could not understand him anyway and who would learn about the hawks soon enough.

If Santiago's ascription of human values to the small bird were felt to be invalid, the literary result would be to present him in the light of a sentimentalist—a romantic of the same sort as the one who wrote: "I fall upon the thorns of life, I bleed." But do discern nobility of being and the lack of it in the creatures of the natural world may, instead, reflect something quite different from the private subjectivity of a sensibility given to sentimentality. It may reflect an awareness which is at once cognizant of the paradoxical existence of realistic fact and idealistic purpose. It is just such a complex awareness that Hemingway has achieved in formulating the character of Santiago. There is an implicit irony in the depiction: the old man is not one who intellectualizes his experience; rather he responds to it with his felt values, with the responses of a simple fisherman. And the validity which we feel in Santiago's responsive judgments and value speculations produces further ramifications of meaning—ones which are quite apart from depiction of Santiago's character. For also implicit is the suggestion of the value character of the universe of being. The small bird who must struggle for its subsistence will presently be confronted with the preying hawks. To the small creature, whose being embodies no malevolence, the old man's response is knowing and sympathetic: " 'Take a good rest, small bird,' he said. 'Then go in and take your chance like any man or bird or fish.' "

When the old man speaks in the first section of going "far out," his concern is with the possibility of catching a "truly big fish." That is, his intention—is the intention of a fisherman—to bring in as large a catch in terms of quantity of fish meat as possible. He reflects that he may not be as strong as he thinks he is, but that he knows many tricks and that he has resolution. But the encounter with the great marlin becomes almost at once something quite different from the mere practical task of bringing in a prize catch for the market. It becomes a contest which transcends practical considerations, one in which the fish takes on an identity which the old man in his humility and wisdom gradually recognizes. His reflections, once the fish has drawn the skiff out of sight of land, emphasize his growing awareness that the nature of this conflict is to be different in kind from the conflict which he had anticipated. At the outset he "regards the fish" with the respect and admiration which, as a fisherman, he has for the prize marlin:

> He is a great fish and I must convince him, he thought. I must never let him learn his strength nor what he could do if he made his run. If I were him I would put in everything now and go until something broke. But, thank God, they are not as intelligent as we who kill them; although they are more noble and more able.

But just as "he loved green turtles and hawks-bills" and just as "he was very fond of flying fish as they were his principal friends on the ocean," he now responds in kind to the fish: "I am with a friend."

Presently the nature of his regard for the fish shifts to an unexpected level and he applies the term he had given to the boy in attempting to account for the essential difference between the practical fisherman and himself: " 'If you're not tired, fish,' he said aloud, 'you must be very strange.' " The struggle, then, becomes more than the struggle of a simple fisherman working at his trade; it becomes, paradoxically, a struggle with a recognized and respected "friend," one who like himself is "strange." It becomes, in short, a struggle of love.

> You are killing me, fish, the old man thought. But you have a right to. Never have I seen a greater, or more beautiful, or a calmer or more noble thing than you, brother. Come on and kill me. I do not care who kills who.
>
> Now you are getting confused in the head, he thought. You must keep your head clear. Keep your head clear and know how to suffer like a man. Or a fish, he thought.

Had Santiago's sphere of existence been determined entirely by materialistic values, there would have been no decision to go "far out." Perhaps the story might have developed from an anecdote which Hemingway reported in an article on the sport of fishing which he had published in the April 1936 *Esquire*, some sixteen years before the publication of *The Old Man and the Sea*.

> Another time an old man fishing alone on a skiff out of Cabanas hooked a great marlin that, on the heavy sashcord handline, pulled the skiff far out to

sea. Two days later the old man was picked up by fishermen sixty miles to the eastward, the head and forward part of the marlin lashed alongside. What was left of the fish, less than half, weighed eight hundred pounds. The old man had stayed with him a day, a night, a day and another night while the fish swam deep and pulled the boat. When he had come up the old man had pulled the boat up on him and harpooned him. Lashed alongside the sharks had hit him and the old man had fought them out alone in the Gulf Stream in a skiff, clubbing them, stabbing at them, lunging at them with an oar until he was exhausted and the sharks had eaten all that they could hold. He was crying in the boat when the fishermen picked him up, half crazy from his loss, and the sharks were still circling the boat.

The story of the old fisherman in the *Esquire* anecdote undoubtedly furnished the germ of the idea for the story of Santiago. Both displayed courage and endurance in sticking tenaciously to their task for two days and nights; both were successful in their struggle with the fish; both fought the sharks until the sharks had destroyed their prize. But the fundamental difference in the two accounts lies in the concept of man underlying each. The old fisherman's story is entirely naturalistic. He is man destroyed, man victimized by environmental forces. When the fish is ruined by the sharks he is left "half crazy from his loss." Santiago's story, on the other hand, is not naturalistic. He is defeated, but only on the level of practical values.

Hemingway's subject matter never involves a mere external conflict; in all of the major short stories and the novels, it involves also an internal conflict, a struggle on the level of being. Santiago's being is much more complex than that of the pathetic figure in the anecdote. The complexity of Santiago's sensibility and his values is most evident in his ability to transcend the vital or subsistence level of his existence. And his reflections suggest a more universal problem, the necessity to destroy what at the same time one loves.

> Then he was sorry for the great fish that had nothing to eat and his determination to kill him never relaxed in his sorrow for him. How many people will he feed, he thought. But are they worthy to eat him? No, of course not. There is no one worthy of eating him from the manner of his behavior and his great dignity. I do not understand these things, he thought. But it is good that we do not have to try to kill the sun or the moon or the stars. It is enough to live on the sea and kill our true brothers.

It is in his values that Santiago has gone "far out"; it is in his values that he is "a strange old man." His questions and speculations would have no relevance for the old fisherman of the anecdote because for him they would simply not exist. The profound difference between what the two fishermen would hold as important is most evident at the point at which Santiago's battle with the fish is won. His victory is a complex one, and, for Hemingway, the complexity defines what an actualized man can be:

> I want to see him, he thought, and to touch and to feel him. He is my fortune, he thought. But that is not why I wish to feel him. I think I felt his heart, he thought. When I pushed on the harpoon shaft the second time.

In the fourth section, the battle with the sharks, going "far out," with all its ramifications for man's existence on the level of being, becomes going "out too far." A new kind of struggle begins with the simple statement, "It was an hour before the first shark hit him," which contains the full sense of the inevitability of those forces which the old man engaged when he had extended the limits and security of the practical world. Hemingway follows the statement with another possessing the same force achieved by his characteristic restraint, saying at once more than could have been said by any other technique: "The shark was not an accident." Now, on the level of being, begins much more than a struggle to retain his prize of fifteen hundred pounds which would "dress out two thirds of that at thirty cents a pound." The struggle with the sharks is a struggle of hate, the counterpart to the struggle of love which had characterized his encounter with the fish. When Santiago drives the harpoon at the oncoming shark, Hemingway formulates the essential difference: "He hit it without hope but with resolution and complete malignancy." And when some forty pounds of the marlin had been torn away, the loss is something different in kind of value from market loss: "He did not like to look at the fish anymore since it had been mutilated. When the fish had been hit it was as though he himself were hit."

Again all levels of subject matter and technique come together when the greater-than-life image of the old man is abruptly brought in contact with the first of the two "hateful" Galanos sharks, those which are "scavengers as well as killers."

> "Ay," he said aloud. There is no translation for this word and perhaps it is just such a noise such as a man might make, involuntarily, feeling the nail go through his hands and into the wood.

The allusion is daring. Its function is to suggest the degree of the pain of recognition when a man with Santiago's capacity for love is confronted with the naked being of malevolence. Hemingway leaves no doubt about the essential nature of these objectifications of malevolence.

It was these sharks that would cut the turtles' legs and flippers off when the turtles were asleep on the surface, and they would hit a man in the water, if they were hungry, even if the man had no smell of fish blood nor of fish slime on him.

Santiago's response is once again a response of being: " 'Ay,' the old man said. 'Galanos. Come on Galanos.' "

In the long struggle to follow, the old man loses the battle to save his fish. But the far more important battle, that which pits the being of the old man against the being of nature's malevolent forces, is not lost. This is the theme of the section. It is stated simply and directly in Santiago's utterance to the sea: "man is not made for defeat"; "A man can be destroyed but not defeated."

In the final short section, the focus shifts to the boy, Manolin. The initial problem, how the boy would once again accompany the old man, is not solved on the practical level of the success or failure of Santiago's venture "far out." Its solution takes place within the being of the boy after the full realization of the old man's experience registers itself upon the boy's sensibility:

He was asleep when the boy looked in the door in the morning. It was blowing so hard that the drifting-boats would not be going out and the boy had slept late and then come to the old man's shack as he had come each morning. The boy saw that the old man was breathing and then he saw the old man's hands and he started to cry. He went out very quietly to go to bring some coffee and all the way down the road he was crying.

Many fishermen were around the skiff looking at what was lashed beside it and one was in the water, his trousers rolled up, measuring the skeleton with a length of line.

The boy did not go down. He had been there before and one of the fishermen was looking after the skiff for him.

"How is he?" one of the fishermen shouted.

"Sleeping," the boy called. He did not care that they saw him crying. "Let no one disturb him."

Thus even though he has failed to bring his fish to market, Santiago's feat has touched a responsive chord in the fishermen of the village. He is once more *El Campeón*. But it is within the boy, because of his deep caring for the old man, that the most significant response occurs. It is a response that resolves the initial problem, at once removing the problem from the level of practical success and placing it on the level of the achievement of being:

"Now we fish together again."

"No, I am not lucky. I am not lucky anymore.

"The hell with luck," the boy said. "I'll bring the luck with me."

The boy's decision recalls a similar decision made by a boy in what Hemingway has called the greatest American novel, *Huckleberry Finn*. There Huck, forced to choose between the demands of a conscience which had been conditioned by the conventions and mores of society to turn over the runaway slave, Jim, and the demands of his own love for Jim as an individual being, declares: "All right, then, I'll go to hell," and makes his decision on the side of being. Like Huck's, Manolin's decision is a recognition of the clashing values of a practical world and the world of individual values. His decision represents the point of his maturity.

In the brief closing scene, the focus is withdrawn in a way that places the drama of conflicting values which defined Santiago's struggle back in the larger context of man's existence in civilized society. For the woman and her companion who belong to the party of tourists who are "at the Terrace looking down in the water among the empty beer cans and dead barracudas," there is no awareness of the kind of drama which is symbolized by the skeleton of the great marlin "that was now just garbage waiting to go out with the tide." They suggest those whose existence is comfortably detached, those who will never "go far out," those for whom the problem of man's being and man's fundamental values is no problem.

6

Bellow's *Seize the Day*

Since 1945 the tradition of naturalism is continued most discernibly in two war novels: James Jones's *From Here to Eternity* and Norman Mailer's *The Naked and the Dead*. Yet the hero of each work is much more complex than the heroes of Dreiser's novels. Each comes to the same ignominious end as Dreiser's characters, but each struggles throughout to maintain a sense of his individual integrity in a world which is not only inimical to individual values but one which has lost the capacity to comprehend them.

But the world of Jones and Mailer was a world of war where the ultimate problem was the problem of physical survival. The writers of the last ten years present a new world and a new problem: in the novels of Salinger, Bellow, Styron, Roth, and Malamud, the dominant theme is man's struggle to discover himself, not merely his psychological self but his ethical self and his religious self. The individual's struggle with the shaping forces of environment is still present, but the problem is infinitely more complex than in its treatment in *Sister Carrie* or *Grapes of Wrath* or *A Farewell to Arms*. For Dreiser and Steinbeck the problem of man was reduced to the terms of the survival of the fittest. For Hemingway, man's problem was how to maintain a stoic self-discipline in a world which was ultimately malevolent. But for Salinger, Bellow, and Malamud, writing after midcentury, there was a new awareness of what individual existence could mean. The problem of man's social and economic existence had given way to a new intellectual and emotional impulse: the individual's determination to discover, amid a welter of inner as well as outer determining forces, a self which could be accepted and affirmed.

What strikes us most forcibly when we reflect on Bellow's *Seize the Day* is the image of the central character, Tommy Wilhelm. Perhaps it is the most significant thing about the novel. If, as its defenders tell us, the chief business of literature is to present images of man that enrich and deepen our insight into the human situation, then this work, I believe, will be recognized as one which captures something essentially valid about man in America at mid-twentieth century.

The narrative line of the story has its interest for us; but what we attend to here is not so much *what happens* to Tommy Wilhelm, as it is his attempt to discover and evaluate himself at first in terms of the values he held while growing up and the effect these values had on his present situation and then in terms of his present values and present relationships.

The opening section presents him as an unmistakable failure: he has lost his job as a salesman; his money is running dangerously low; his wife, from whom he is separated, hounds him without mercy for money; his father, a retired successful physician, has little respect for him, and Tommy is about to enter into a stock market venture with a man whom he fearfully suspects of being a charlatan. We see him living alone in a hotel inhabited by people like his father, who have passed the age of retirement. His most immediate problem is that of presenting a mask of the respectable businessman.

The opening lines present not only his predicament but suggest something of his attitude toward it:

When it came to concealing his troubles, Tommy Wilhelm was not less capable than the next fellow. So at least he thought, and there was a certain amount of evidence to back him up. He had once been an actor—no, not quite, an extra—and he knew what acting should be. Also, he was smoking a cigar, and when a man is smoking a cigar, wearing a hat, he has an advantage; it is harder to find out how he feels.

Vaguely implicit in the passage is the suggestion that the wearing of a mask reflects not so much on the individual who presents it as it does on a society which requires it—a society conditioned to discern the failure or the misfit, and prompt in its rejection of him.

Bellow's presentation of Tommy Wilhelm, virtually alone and out of work, coming down to the hotel lobby compelled to follow a kind of desperate fiction that the daily routine of the prosperous businessman was an unquestioned necessity, is immediately reminiscent of Dreiser's Hurstwood or Arthur Miller's Willy Loman:

And for several months, because he had no position, he had kept up his morale by rising early; he was shaved and in the lobby by eight o'clock. He bought the paper and some cigars and drank a Coca-Cola or two before he went in to breakfast with his father. After breakfast—out, out, out to attend to business. The getting out had in itself become the chief business. But he had realized that he could not keep this up much longer, and today he was afraid. He was aware that his routine was about to break up and he sensed that a huge trouble long presaged but till now formless was due.

But the similarity to Hurstwood and to Willy Loman is a superficial one. Hurstwood and Willy Loman are images of man destroyed by environmental forces; the inevitable end in both of these naturalistic accounts is defeat and suicide. Tommy Wilhelm experiences the same destructive misfortunes; he is wiped out in a momentary fluctuation of the stock market: "He could see for himself that the electronic bookkeeping device must have closed him out." He is betrayed by the only person he had reached out to for friendship. And he is rejected with a finality by his father when he appeals to him for sympathetic understanding: "But one word from you, just a word, would go a long way." And then presently: " 'Father, listen! Listen.' " His father's response is the final blow: " 'Go away from me now. It's torture for me to look at you, you slob.' "

But Tommy Wilhelm's end is not the end of a pathetic victim of naturalistic forces. The real subject matter of the novel is much more complex. And the final image of Tommy Wilhelm can be understood only in the light of the deeper subject matter that Bellow is concerned with.

The key to the understanding of the deeper meanings of the novel does not lie in the social and economic failures of the novel's central figure. As Melville's Ahab put it, we must look again, and at one level lower. We see that behind all of his social aspirations and economic ambitions lies a driving need to be recognized. And what is singular is that it is not social and economic recognition that he really seeks; it is recognition from his father. We see that Tommy Wilhelm's most basic emotion is his love for his father. He reflects:

> If he was poor, I could care for him and show it. The way I *could* care, too, if I only had a chance. He'd see how much love and respect I had in me. It would make him a different man, too. He'd put his hands on me and give me his blessing.

And when the mercenary charlatan who poses as a psychologist, Dr. Tamkin, questions him about his possible inheritance from his aging father, Tommy's reply again reveals his real concern in his relationship with his father:

> "When I get desperate—of course I think about money. But I don't want anything to happen to him. I certainly don't want him to die." Tamkin's brown eyes glittered shrewdly at him. "You don't believe it. Maybe it's not psychological. But on my word of honor. A joke is a joke, but I don't want to joke about stuff like this. When he dies, I'll be robbed, like. I'll have no more father."

And when Dr. Tamkin, in the hardened manner characteristic of the opportunist, asks, "You love your old man?" Tommy's response is central to what is most fundamental in him as a man:

> Wilhelm grasped at this. "Of course, of course I love him. My father. My mother—" As he said this there was a great pull at the very center of his soul. When a fish strikes the line you feel the live force in your hand. A mysterious being beneath the water, driven by hunger, has taken the hook and rushes away and fights, writhing. Wilhelm never identified what struck within him.

Bellow works carefully and long with the relationship between father and son. When Tommy, who has changed his name from Adler to Wilhelm, tries to engage his father's feelings for his unhappy state, Dr. Adler suggests steam baths and exercise and stoically keeps himself detached from his son. And Wilhelm reflects:

> He wants a young, smart, successful son,—and he said, "Oh, Father, it's nice of you to give me this medical advice, but steam isn't going to cure what ails me." The doctor measurably drew back.

We finally realize that the father maintains his detachment from his son by the device of rejecting Tommy's behavior. Yet it is evident that the real rejection is not of behavior; rather it is a rejection of Tommy himself.

But just as Bellow's real subject matter is not the naturalist's theme of the social and economic failure of a son, so also his subject matter is not merely a psychological case history. The ultimate consideration of the novel is a moral one. It concerns the human condition, the problem of the meaning of man's humanity in the world of the mid-twentieth century.

To understand Dr. Adler's cold detachment from his son's misery, one must understand the essential nature of Dr. Tamkin, who stands as a symbol for the new man of a new age of opportunism. Here is Bellow's presentation of what man has become in a world which gives its most real admiration to the image of success. Dr. Tamkin, the self-declared psychologist, who has mastered the techniques of making profits from the stock market, is presented as the socially genial, well-adjusted man about town, his life well ordered and his judgments quick and precise. He is at no time troubled as Tommy Wilhelm is troubled. Perhaps it is precisely here that what is most essential to his nature resides. For we finally feel that Bellow is saying that to possess a sense of humanity is necessarily to be troubled. Dr. Tamkin's adjustment, we realize, is a mechanically frightening one. He is a man who had learned the weaknesses of the human condition and who puts his knowledge to practical use. He is presented as not only devoid of sympathetic understanding but as one for whom the possibility of it has ceased to exist.

Bellow's image of Dr. Tamkin is one of the most singular condemnations in contemporary literature of what modern man has become. From his voice come some of the most profound and incisive insights of the

novel. When Wilhelm questions him about his practice
of psychology, Dr. Tamkin's reply reveals the keenness
of his mentality:

> "And you do psychological work with your own
> friends? I didn't know that was allowed."
>
> "Well, I'm a radical in the profession. I have to do
> good wherever I can."
>
> . . . .
>
> "With me," said Dr. Tamkin, "I'm at my most
> efficient when I don't need the fee. When I only love.
> Without a financial reward. I remove myself from
> the social influence. Especially money. The spiritual
> compensation is what I look for. Bringing people
> into the here-and-now. The real universe. That's the
> present moment. The past is no good to us. The fu-
> ture is full of anxiety. Only the present is real—the
> here-and-now. Seize the day."

For Dr. Tamkin, influencing people is an art and
winning friends has a method to it. We see him throughout as the master of manipulation and calculation, the
possessor of keen insight, yet for whom insight is not a
moral achievement but a tool. In his relationship with
Tommy Wilhelm he doesn't reach to Tommy's deeper
levels of awareness in order to help him or to share his
feelings as a friend. Rather he wishes, by what he has
become in his essential nature, to use and manipulate
him to his own interests. Dr. Tamkin's intellectual interest in psychological and philosophical insight is
valid enough. But it is the kind of moral man behind
that interest that gives his insight its direction. Some
of his judgments seem breathtaking in their precision
and perspicacity. But Bellow's point is that here is a
new creature—a new product of a new age—spawned
by that age, its necessary offspring, who uses his intellectual achievement as an instrument.

We feel that people like Tommy's father, who has chosen a New York hotel for the place of his retirement, must necessarily develop a hardened and detached attitude when confronted in the daily round of living with the ever-present menace of the city's Dr. Tamkins. Unable to alter what he has become in his defense against being taken in—suspicious, aloof, detached— Dr. Adler rejects his son's troubles. His son has allowed himself to become the victim of his own bad judgments. Yet in rejecting his son's behavior and his faulty judgments—"I want nobody on my back. Get off! And I give you the same advice, Wilky. Carry nobody on your back"—in rejecting his son's troubles, Dr. Adler, ironically, rejects his own humanity. But it is a rejection which does not come out of a reflective decision. We realize Dr. Adler's response possesses an automatic quality. It has its source in the nature of the man he has become.

It is a final irony of the novel that the one person who clings to the reality of what it means to be human is, in the eyes of his world, a misfit. Yet we feel that it is precisely in his possession of a sense of humanity that Tommy Wilhelm does not emerge a defeated man, a pathetic victim of forces beyond his control. In a climactic scene in which Tommy Wilhelm sits watching the market fluctuations which presently would wipe out his remaining money, he reflects on the human condition that *is* his world:

That sick Mr. Perls at breakfast had said that there was no easy way to tell the sane from the mad, and he was right about that in any big city and especially in New York—the end of the world, with its complexity and machinery, bricks and tubes, wires and stones, holes and heights. And was everybody crazy here? What sort of people did you see? Every other man spoke a language entirely his own, which he had figured out by private thinking; he had his own ideas and peculiar ways.

And presently:

> You had to translate and translate, explain and explain, back and forth, and it was the punishment of hell itself not to understand or be understood, not to know the crazy from the sane, the wise from the fools, the young from the old or the sick from the well. The fathers were no fathers and the sons no sons. You had to talk with yourself in the daytime and reason with yourself at night. Who else was there to talk to in a city like New York?

If Bellow's hero had concluded his reflections here, his judgments would indeed be the judgments of a defeated Hurstwood or Willy Loman. But Bellow's concept of man is not that of Dreiser or Arthur Miller. As Tommy Wilhelm continues his reflections we see the essential difference:

> He went several degrees further—when you are like this, dreaming that everybody is outcast, you realize that this must be one of the small matters. There is a larger body, and from this you cannot be separated.

The idea of this larger body had been planted in him a few days ago beneath Times Square:

> He was going through an underground corridor, a place he had always hated and hated more than ever now. On the walls between the advertisements were words in chalk: "Sin No More," and "Do Not Eat the Pig," he had particularly noticed. And in the dark tunnel, in the haste, heat, and darkness which disfigure and make freaks and fragments of nose and eyes and teeth, all of a sudden, unsought, a general love for all these imperfect and lurid-looking people burst out in Wilhelm's breast. He loved them. One

and all, he passionately loved them. They were his
brothers and his sisters. He was imperfect and dis-
figured himself, but what difference did that make if
he was united with them by this blaze of love? And
as he walked he began to say, "Oh my brothers—
my brothers and my sisters," blessing them all as
well as himself.

In Salinger's *Franny and Zooey*, the same kind of
experienced acceptance of all mankind is the central
theme of the novel. Salinger approaches his theme
through subject matter which is essentially religious,
and his final artistic judgment is religious in nature.
Again, in Malamud's *The Assistant*, the central theme is
the final awareness by the protagonist that in the realiz-
able love of his fellow man lies the meaning of human
existence. Again the approach is religious, in Malamud
in terms of the Jewish religious tradition, in Salinger in
terms of the Christian tradition.

Interestingly enough, although Bellow nowhere al-
ludes to religious subject matter in presenting his theme
of man's acceptance of man, the significant meaning
of the novel parallels the meanings in Salinger's *Franny
and Zooey* and Malamud's *The Assistant*.

In the final scene of *Seize the Day*, Tommy Wilhelm,
while searching for the absconded Dr. Tamkin, catches
sight of him among a crowd of people in front of a
funeral parlor. Tommy finds himself pressed by the
crowd, which is being herded by a policeman, into the
interior of the funeral parlor where he is confronted by
the open coffin. His response to seeing the stranger in
the coffin embodies Bellow's central theme that the
meaning in human existence resides finally in man's
capacity for and sense of humanity.

But within a few minutes he had forgotten Tamkin. He stood along the wall with others and looked
toward the coffin and the slow line that was moving

past it, gazing at the face of the dead. Presently he too was in this line, and slowly, slowly, foot by foot, the beating of his heart anxious, thick, frightening, but somehow also rich, he neared the coffin and paused for his turn, and gazed down. He caught his breath when he looked at the corpse, and his face swelled, his eyes shone hugely with instant tears.

The dead man was gray-haired. He had two large waves of gray hair at the front. But he was not old. His face was long, and he had a bony nose, slightly, delicately twisted. His brows were raised as though he had sunk into final thought. Now at last he was with it, after the end of all distractions, and when his flesh was no longer flesh. And by this meditative look Wilhelm was so struck that he could not go away. In spite of the tinge of horror, and then the splash of heartsickness that he felt, he could not go. He stepped out of line and remained beside the coffin; his eyes filled silently and through his still tears he studied the man as the line of visitors moved with veiled looks past the satin coffin toward the standing bank of lilies, lilacs, roses. With great stifling sorrow, almost admiration, Wilhelm nodded and nodded. On the surface, the dead man with his formal shirt and his tie and silk lapels and his powdered skin looked so proper; only a little beneath so—black, Wilhelm thought, so fallen in the eyes.

Standing a little apart, Wilhelm began to cry. He cried at first softly and from sentiment, but soon from deeper feeling.

. . . .

The great knot of illness and grief in his throat swelled upward and he gave in utterly and held his face and wept.

Tommy Wilhelm's grief is, of course, grief for mankind, grief for the human situation. Thus, the real story of Tommy Wilhelm is not the story of modern man, victimized by the forces of his environment or even the mercenary values of his environment. We sense that in his capacity for grief for humanity lies the possibility of his freedom from being determined by his environment. Tommy is, indeed, neurotic in his anxieties, in his obsession with his concern about his father's regard, in his strivings for success and recognition. And at middle age, overweight, graying and unkempt, he presents a strange hero. Yet in his singular way he is free where the others are not free, now in his final failure, from the phoniness of the charlatans, from the uncertainty of the closed lines of the masked faces. We feel that in the openness of his grief is a new realization of his role. There is no concern here with what was his chief concern at the beginning—that of concealing, of presenting the mask of something he wasn't. And for Bellow, it is his humanity which makes possible his freedom.

Yet Saul Bellow's image of man is hardly the image traditionally suggested by the various forms of humanism. For what Bellow offers is not so much an image of what man, in spite of life's vicissitudes and frustrations, can be. Rather, what Bellow presents is the image of man which emerges from the discovery of self when that self encounters the vicissitudes, frustrations, and anxieties of living existence.

Such an image suggests no preconceptions about living life or developing the self; rather it expresses a confidence in the basic nature of man, in particular, man caught in the dehumanizing forces of mid-twentieth century existence

It is an image of man involved in living life—one whose whole being is engaged, whose convictions are *discovered* by himself in the process of encountering and responding to his daily existence.

7

Malamud's *The Fixer*

Although the germ of the idea for *The Fixer* is undoubtedly the actual arrest and trial of one Mendel Beiliss, a Russian Jew who was accused of a ritual murder, it would be a mistake to see Malamud's work as essentially an historical account. The point is that we are not so much concerned with the events of Yakov Bok's imprisonment as we are with his responses to those events. *The Fixer* may indeed resemble "an historical novel" but it does so because it presents the history of a developing sensibility, of the fundamental change within an individual whose struggle for freedom to be a human being has been from the beginning a personal quest, however dimly realized by the protagonist, for release from his own inner imprisonment.

What is perhaps most distinctive about Malamud's novel is that its subject matter is concerned with two stories which evolve simultaneously. Both stories involve the conflict of imprisonment and freedom but in quite different ways. The first is the story of the unjust imprisonment of Yakov Bok, ostensibly for the ritual murder of a Christian boy; the presentations here, i.e., the narrative images, the scenes, and the episodes embody Yakov's miserable lot in prison and his continual struggle for his release. The second story is of the imprisonment of Yakov Bok's psychological and moral self. The images, scenes, and episodes here present his generally unfree state of being and his gradual emergence from that spiritual confinement. Thus like Malamud's earlier novel, *The Assistant* (1957), *The Fixer* is centrally concerned with the existential being of the central character. That is, like Camus's *The Stranger*, a novel also about an imprisonment, *The Fixer* is focused thematically more on revealing the nature of an individual existence than on the dramatic events of an imprisonment. And like Malamud's *A New Life* (1961), its theme is the protagonist's discovery that what is most significant about a new life resides within man himself and begins with his capacity for his own inner freedom. In that work, the central character, Levin, declares: "I suddenly knew, as though I was discovering it for the first time that the source of freedom is the human spirit."

My intention is not to minimize the dramatic narration of the events of *The Fixer*. Clearly the story of Yakov's imprisonment is a poignant and detailed story of human suffering—a continual suffering made more intense not merely by cold, privation, and physical pain but by ever-increasing isolation from human communication. But again, the focus is not so much on the dramatic quality of Yakov's suffering as it is upon the meaning and significance of his suffering. And it is this focus that removes *The Fixer* from possible classification as a naturalistic novel. Such a reading would be in error. Malamud's hero is indeed victimized by the forces of his cultural environment, forces over which he has no control. But the Yakov Bok whose suffering has meant a discovery of new limits to what it means to be a human being can hardly be regarded as a pathetic victim. And although *The Fixer* is unquestionably an affirmative novel, what is affirmed is man's struggle itself—as the given, the fundamental norm of his existence and at the same time the possibility of his free response to his condition. Bibikov, the kindly investigating magistrate, in a conversation with the fixer gives the earliest statement of the theme, which suggests something of its universality as a contemporary archetype:

> One often feels helpless in the face of the confusion of these times, such a mass of apparently uncontrollable events and experiences to live through, attempt to understand, and if at all possible, give order to; but one must not withdraw from the task if he has some small thing to offer—he does so at the risk of diminishing his humanity.

Thus each of Malamud's three major novels is concerned, I believe, with the *being* of the central character, with his decision to discover a new life, with the subject matter of the search, which in every case begins with the search for self. And in each novel, despite ironies, usually ludicrous, the hero succeeds—never, however in the terms in which he had envisioned his quest.

Like Frank Alpine of *The Assistant,* who makes a decision to change his life and unwittingly begins with participation in robbery and assault, and like Sy Levin, who crosses the country in search of *A New Life,* Yakov Bok leaves the shtetl "to get acquainted with a bit of the world," "to know what's going on in the world." And like Frank Alpine and Sy Levin, Yakov does not realize that underlying the decision is an impulse stronger than his ability to account for it intellectually. In each novel the decision for change is gradually revealed to the consciousness of the hero as the beginning of a quest, not merely for a new life in a new environment but for a new life in a new free self.

At the outset, Yakov, though an unusual "fixer"— one who carries *Selections from Spinoza* with his bag of tools—is characterized by his disappointment with his lot. All of the images in the opening section reveal an attitude toward his life of dissatisfaction and disillusionment.

> I've had to dig with my fingernails for a living. What can anybody do without capital? What they can do I can do but it's not much. I fix what's broken—except in the heart. In this shtetl everything is falling apart.

It is clear that Yakov Bok as viewpoint character is much more than a convention for telling the story; rather his assertions function dramatically to present his sensibility. We see what it is that this sensibility focuses on and how open it is and how restricted—a matter of the relative freedom or unfreedom of his psychological and moral self. And presently we see his characteristic touch of whimsical humor that is part of his attitude toward the events of his life—a touch of humor that suggests the possibility of a free spirit, an inherent potential to detach himself from his troubles. But during the time of his departure from the shtetl, the overwhelming reality about Yakov's character is his spiritual unfreedom: his bitterness and general dissatisfaction with his lot. He is bitter about his unfaithful wife, Raisl, "He cursed her when he thought of her." He reflects that she "couldn't get pregnant in five and a half years. She bore me no children so who could I look in the eye? And now she runs off with some stranger she met at the inn—a goy I'm positive." As he leaves the protected life of the Jewish community, the shtetl, he laments, "all I have to my name after thirty years in this graveyard is sixteen rubles that I got from selling everything I own." And he views his life as generally meaningless, as completely lacking in significance:

he blamed fate and spared himself. His nervousness

showed in his movements. Generally he moved faster than he had to, considering how little there was to do, but he was always doing something. After all, he was a fixer and had to keep his hands busy.

Further, the images of the Yakov Bok who leaves the shtetl for Kiev are the images of a man full of anxiety:

The horse had slowed down again, a black year on its stupid head. Suppose those clouds, grown dark and heavy, cracked open on their undersides and poured snow upon the world. Would the horse make it?

Throughout the journey his state of unfreedom defines the world of his most real existence:

He was afraid he might be robbed of his few rubles so he stayed put and made uncertain progress. The sky was thick with stars, the wind blowing cold in his face. Once he slept momentarily and woke in shivering sweat from a nightmare.

Yet his fears are presented as ludicrous and without foundation:

By then it was pitch dark. The wind boomed. The steppe was a black sea full of strange voices. Here nobody spoke Yiddish, and the nag, maybe feeling the strangeness of it, began to trot and soon came close to flight. . . . Ghosts rose like smoke in the Ukraine. From time to time he felt a presence at his back but would not turn. . . . Once he slept momentarily and woke in a shivering sweat from a nightmare.

Even after his arrival at his destination, Yakov's state of mind prevents any desire he may have had to be present to the world he had struggled to achieve, i.e.,

Malamud presents him as only partially free to be open to his experience:

> Kiev, "the Jerusalem of Russia," still awed and disquieted him. He had been there for a few hot summer days after being conscripted into the army, and now, again, he saw it with *half the self*—the other half worried about his worries. [Italics mine]

And in his new environment, as an overseer in the brickyard, what is most real to him is his continued troubled self:

> In the dark he feared calamities he only occasionally thought of during the day—the stable in flames, burning down with him in it, bound hand and foot unable to move; and the maddened horses destroying themselves. Or dying of consumption, or syphilis, coughing up or pissing blood. And he dreaded what worried him most—to be unmasked as a hidden Jew. "Gevalt!" he shouted, then listened in fright for sounds in the stable to tell him whether the drivers were there and had heard him cry out.

This, then, is the Yakov Bok before he is imprisoned—an individual blocked from his experience by his state of being and distorting even the simplest experience of the objective world. He is a man leading a half-life in his frustrations, anxieties, and formless fears. Malamud is thorough in his formulation of the Yakov Bok of the opening sections. The formulation is essential to the developing theme of the novel. Ironically, Yakov states it when he attempts to explain what reading Spinoza meant to him: "what I think it means is that he was out to make a free man out of himself." But at this point Yakov's understanding of freedom is purely intellectual—an abstraction from his reading of *Selections from Spinoza*. The assertions of Yakov, expressing his fears, give the work the direction of forthcoming personal catastrophe in the promise of some unknown disastrous situation, which indeed develops. Yet there is a profound irony in formal meaning here: what is not suggested in his utterances of anxiety is that the real direction of the work is not to lie in Yakov's "fate"; rather it is to lie in his state of being.

One of Yakov's chief characteristics from the outset is an impulse to reflection about events, reflection that leads to his own awareness of his own weaknesses. When after two and a half years in a cell, Yakov reflects on his imprisonment, on "Why?," his reflections are not calculated to throw light on the events in the manner of an omniscient viewpoint character. Rather, his reflections function to present, perhaps to objectify in T. S. Eliot's sense, something of the essential nature, the inner reality of Yakov Bok:

> It had happened [the imprisonment]—he was back to this again—because he was Yakov Bok and had an extraordinary amount to learn. He had learned, it wasn't easy; the experience was his; it was worse than that, it was he. He was the experience. It also meant that now he was somebody else than he had been, who would have thought it.

The passage is at once an expression of his propensity to be an aware man, to stand apart from his experience and see it in its larger context. And presently, after reflecting on the value of his awareness, he admits that what he has learned will not help him get out of prison. Then he concludes: "Still, it was better than not knowing. A man had to learn, it was his nature." Malamud's focus here, as everywhere in the novel, is not on the objective event, but on the knowing subject. And it is in the reader's experiencing the experience of this responding subject, who is involved in the most significant of all human processes, that of the discovery of the free self, that the dramatic quality of the work resides.

And at each stage of his developing consciousness, the revelation of what is happening occurs because Malamud's heroes characteristically possess reflective minds. Even in the unfreedom of his fears, Yakov is a man given to reflection. When, for example, he arrives in Kiev, the destination he had sought in leaving "the prison" in the shtetl, he is still a fearful man, yet one who can stand apart momentarily from his fears in his awareness of them:

> He went where he had not been before, speaking in Russian to anyone who spoke to him—testing himself, he explained it to himself. Why should a man be afraid of the world? Because he was, if for no other reason.

And although he is presented as a man who sees his new environment "with half the self," yet he is at the same time characterized as a man who is never completely blocked from living. That is, he is shown to be, however paradoxical the presentation, a man for whom the potential to be open to life is always present. His responses to concrete happenings reveal from the outset his underlying conviction that the real meaning of life resides in the daily fact of living it, and he is presented as eagerly reaching out for just this meaning:

> Still, as he wandered from street to street, the colors were light and pretty. A golden haze hung in the air in the late afternoons. The busy avenues were full of people, among them Ukrainian peasants in their native dress, gypsies, soldiers, priests. At night the white gas globes glowed in the streets and there were thick mists on the river. Kiev stood on three hills, and he remembered his first trembling sight of the

city from the Nicholas Bridge—dotted with white houses with green roofs, churches and monasteries, their gold and silver domes floating above the green foliage. He wasn't without an eye for a pretty scene, though that added nothing to his living. Still, a man was more than a workhorse, or so they said.

And Malamud never loses sight of the complexity which he has developed in his overall image of his hero. Even in the midst of Yakov's terror following his arrest and questioning, he retains the possibility of momentary freedom from his troubled self to experience his world:

> "You," [Grubeshov] said to Yakov, who was gazing out the window at the rain in the chestnut trees, "you know well this concerns you so pay attention." In the time the fixer had been in prison the city had turned green and there were sweet smelling lilacs everywhere but who could enjoy them? Through the open window he could smell the wet grass and new leaves, and where the cemetery ended there were birches with silver trunks.

The passage is important in the thematic construction of the work. Seen as a bit of description by an omniscient author, with an authorial aside on the sweet-smelling lilacs, i.e., "but who could enjoy them?," the technique resembles Dreiser's technique in his early naturalistic work, *Sister Carrie*. But seen as a formulation of the sensibility of the viewpoint character, the passage more nearly resembles Joyce's expressionistic intention in the presentation of the character of Gabriel Conroy or even Leopold Bloom. Like Joyce's, Malamud's focus is on the complex presentation of the psychological and moral being of his central character.

The theme of the freedom of the human spirit as a necessary condition for living appears in three distinct conflicts in Yakov's life: in his capacity to be open to the world of his daily existence apart from his relationship to it; in his capacity to be open to human relationships apart from his needs in the relationship; and in his capacity to commit himself through political action to a cause in the community of man. The first concerns his ability to celebrate the quality of the real world around him; the second concerns his ability to celebrate not another but rather the reality of a relationship with another; the third concerns his ability to celebrate his experienced relationship with mankind. In each instance the problem for Yakov is presented as vitally connected to the problem of freedom. His homespun answer to Bibikov's question—a key thematic image—concerning Spinoza's views on the source of freedom objectifies the relationship between freedom of the human spirit and the fulfillment of human living: "It's as though a man flies over his head on the wings of reason, or some such thing. You join the universe and forget your worries."

Yakov's struggle to be a free man begins in his vaguely understood but powerfully felt impulse to leave the world of the Jewish community, first the shtetl where he had spent his entire life and presently the Podol, the Jewish community in Kiev, where he was required by Russian law to live. All of his utterances in an early scene in the shtetl presenting his relationship with his father-in-law, Shmuel, express a strong desire to abandon the life of withdrawal from the world conflicts, however relatively secure that withdrawal, and go out into the world. When Shmuel argues with his decision to leave the shtetl—"but what I don't understand is why you want to bother with Kiev. It's a dangerous city full of churches and anti-Semites"—Yakov's answer is unequivocal:

"I've been cheated from the start," Yakov said bitterly. "What I've been through personally you know already, not to mention living here all my life except for a few months in the army. The shtetl is a prison, no change from the days of Khmelnitsky. It moulders and the Jews moulder in it. Here we're all prisoners, I don't have to tell you, so it's time to try elsewhere I've finally decided. I want to make a living. I want to get acquainted with a bit of the world. I've read a few books in recent years and it's surprising what goes on that none of us knows about."

It is, of course, an irony in the light of his imprisonment that Yakov wishes to leave the shtetl because "the shtetl is a prison." Yet it is a deeper irony that the peaceful life of the shtetl would indeed prevent him from getting "acquainted with a bit of the world," i.e., we see that it is finally only in going out of the shtetl that he finds the meaning in his life that he vaguely seeks. And presently within the same scene, the rejection of withdrawal is again emphasized, this time in terms of internal rather than external freedom. To Yakov's assertion, "What I want to know is what's going on in the world," Shmuel argues, "That's all in the Torah, there's no end to it. Stay away from the wrong books, Yakov, the impure." But Yakov has formed some convictions on the matter, however untested: "there are no wrong books. What's wrong is the fear of them."

We see that the impulse in Yakov, however objectified primarily in intellectual pronouncements, is to be free of fears and superstition. Yet as soon as he has left the shtetl, his first experience is fear and anxiety. And although his specific fears are in fact largely formless—the "snowstorm" (that doesn't materialize), the "fog," the "darkening steppe," "ghostly presences at his back," "being robbed"—yet to go out into the world, however necessary if one is to take up the business of human living, is at the same time justifiable cause for anxiety. As Yakov reflects in one of the closing scenes: "Your afflictions were from life—a poor living, mistakes with people, the blows of fate."

What the novel finally affirms is that the freedom to live is not merely the freedom to experience, but also ironically the freedom to struggle and even to suffer. The point is made specifically when Yakov's reading of the Old Testament brings his own discovery, one quite different in emphasis from the traditional interpretations of the gentle Shmuel:

> The purpose of the covenant, Yakov thinks, is to create human experience, although human experience baffles God. God is after all God; what he is is what he is: God. What does he know about such things? Has he ever worshipped God? Has he ever suffered? How much, after all, has he experienced? God envies the Jews: it's a rich life. Maybe He would like to be human, it's possible.

What Yakov sees the Old Testament present becomes for him a new insight into just what it is that differentiates man's experience as uniquely man's. And in his characteristic whimsical manner, his insight develops into a realization of a major limitation in the nature of the God of the Old Testament, namely that God cannot be a human being:

> Then he read longer and faster, gripped by the narrative of the joyous and frenzied Hebrews, doing business, fighting wars, sinning and worshipping— whatever they were doing always engaged in talk with the huffing-puffing God who tried to sound, maybe out of envy, like a human being.

The passage, I think, reflects, in spite of Yakov's whimsy, one aspect of the concept of man upon which the novel is based, namely that the living of life, including its struggling and suffering, is not simply the fate of man but the privilege of man. There is, however, no suggestion that the affirmation of human living as the embodiment of suffering and struggle implies a masochistic seeking after suffering. As Yakov pointedly remarks in his imaginary dialogue with the Tsar: "Excuse me, Your Majesty, but what suffering has taught me is the uselessness of suffering." Rather in *The Fixer* it is the seeking after *living* that is affirmed, and in Malamud's theme, one undeniable characteristic of human living *is* human suffering: "You lived, you suffered, but you lived."

The extent of Yakov Bok's suffering is given the fullest possible development by Malamud. The narrative images, scenes, and episodes which present Yakov's miserable condition through two and one half years of imprisonment constitute a major part of the experience of the novel. Gradually we see that it is not the suffering itself that is the central concern here; rather it is the implications of the suffering that are uppermost thematically. The repeated attempts to force a confession of guilt from Yakov in order to bring support to the failure to develop sufficient evidence to bring him to trial intensifies his suffering but gives it, of course, a deeper political implication. Some of Malamud's most powerful writing is to be found in these presentations. Much of the power, I think, comes from the technique of presenting the subject matter of the imprisonment through the viewpoint character's eyes, but in Malamud's unique manner, one which seems to use the free range of the omniscient author's vision, which at the same time is always tied back to the sensibility of the character himself: "When one had nothing to do the worst thing to have was an endless supply of minutes. It was like pouring nothing into a million little bottles." Or again, in an image of Yakov's desperate pacing, which is his first response to his fear that "he might go crazy doing nothing," that "he hadn't the wit, he told himself, to be this much alone":

> He walked all day and into the night, until his shoes fell apart, and then walked in his bare feet on the lacerating floor. He walked in almost liquid heat with nowhere to go but his circular entrapment, striking himself on his journey—his chest, face, head, tearing his flesh, lamenting his life.
>
> His crooked feet hurt unbearably. Yakov lay down in exhaustion on the floor. Torture by his own instrument—pain of body on deep depression.

We see that Yakov's imprisonment in these early months is intensified by his own physical response to his despair, that he is also a prisoner of his own troubled self. These then are the narrative images which present the period of Yakov's greatest unfreedom, the time of his complete entrapment in his suffering:

> Time was summer now, when the hot cell stank heavily and the walls sweated. There were mosquitoes, and bugs hitting the walls. Yet, better summer; he feared another winter. And if there was a spring after the winter it would mean two years in prison. And after that? Time blew like a steppe wind into an empty future. There was no end, no event, indictment, trial. The waiting withered him. He was worn thin by the struggle to wait, by the knowledge of his innocence against the fact of his imprisonment; that nothing had been done in a whole year to free him. He was stricken to be so absolutely alone. Oppressed by the heat, eaten by damp cold, eroded by the expectation of an indictment that never came, were his gray bones visible through his skin? His nerves were threads stretched to the instant before

snapping. He cried out of the deepest part of him, a narrow pit, but no one appeared or answered, or looked at him or spoke to him, neither friend nor stranger.

It is at this point that Yakov's situation begins, almost imperceptively at first, to undergo a fundamental change; he begins to experience moments of release from his misery. The first indication of his new desire to live is in his new interest in food—not for subsistence merely but for the enjoyment of the experience of eating:

> The minute after he had eaten he was hungry. He had visions of Zhitnyak appearing one day with a huge plate of well-seasoned chicken soup, thick with broad yellow noodles, a platter of meat kreplach, and half a haleh loaf from which he would tear hunks of sweet foamy bread that melted on the tongue. He dreamed of rice and noodle pudding with raisins and cinnamon, as Raisl had deliciously baked it; and of anything that went with sour cream—blintzes, cheese kreplach, boiled potatoes, radishes, scallions, sliced crisp cucumbers. Also of juicy tomatoes of tremendous size that he had seen in Viscover's kitchen. He sucked a ripe tomato till it dribbled from his mouth, then, to get to sleep, finally had to finish it off, thickly salted, with a piece of white bread.

And then the imagined experience is transferred at once to a real experience as Yakov gives conscious form to the experience. His action reflects an existential decision to come out of his withdrawal in his miserable suffering in order once again to experience his experience:

> After such fantasies he could hardly wait for the guard to come with his breakfast; yet when it came

at last he restrained himself, eating very slowly. First
he chewed the bread until its hard texture and grain
flavor were gone, then bit by bit swallowed it down.
Usually he saved part of his ration for nighttime, in
bed, when he got ravenously hungry thinking of food.
After the bread he ate the gruel, sucking each barley
grain as it melted in his mouth. At night he worked
every spoonful of soup over his tongue, each pulpy
cabbage bit and thread of meat, taking it in very
small sips and swallows, at the end scraping the bowl
with his blackened spoon.

The point is that at such moments his focus is not on
his desperate situation; rather for such moments he is
free from the imprisonment of his suffering. As his zest
for food continues in a zest for living generally, he uses
every device available to him to pursue his new sense of
being alive: he reads the newspapers which were given
to him to clean himself; he recalls fragments of psalms
and recites them aloud; he makes efforts to remember
things he had read, especially incidents from the life of
Spinoza, and he reflects, "[Spinoza] was free in his
thoughts." Then in a new section, marked "7" in chapter 6, in which Malamud shifts the viewpoint to the
second person, Yakov begins to employ Spinoza's concept
of freedom as a device for securing his own: he envisions the possibility of moments of freedom from
his misery by attempting to create concrete experiences
which he could experience in his imagined construc-
tions:

You wait. You wait in minutes of hope and days of
hopelessness. Sometimes you just wait, there's no
greater insult. You sink into your thoughts and try
to blot out the prison cell. (If you're lucky it dissolves and you spend a half hour out in the open,
beyond the doors and walls and the hatred of your-

self.) If you're lucky and get out to the shtetl you
might call on a friend, or if he's out, sit along on a
bench in front of his hut. You can smell the grass and
the flowers and look at the girls, if one or two happen
to be passing by along the road. You can also do a
day's work if there's work to do. Today there's a little
carpentering job. You work up a sweat sawing wood
apart and hammering it together. When it's time to
eat you open your food parcel—not bad. The thing
about food is to have a little when you want it. A
hard-boiled egg with a pinch of salt is delicious. Also
some sour cream with a cut-up potato. If you dip
bread into fresh milk and suck before swallowing, it
tastes like a feast. And hot tea with lemon and a
lump of sugar. In the evening you go across the wet
grass to the edge of the wood. You stare at the moon
in the milky sky. You breathe in the fresh air. An
ambition teases you, there's still the future. After all,
you're alive and free. Even if you're not so free, you
think you are. The worst thing about such thoughts
is when they leave you and you're back in the
cell. The cell is your woods and sky.

The passage is an important one in the development of
Malamud's central theme: The freedom of the self
from itself—evident in one's capacity to see, to experience, and to celebrate the objective world—is the
first and most necessary step in the freeing of the human spirit, without which, in Malamud's vision, there
is no possibility for human living itself. Malamud presents Yakov's first task as that of coming "out in the
open, beyond the doors and walls and the hatred of
yourself." And "if you're lucky" the prison cell and the
prison of the "hatred of yourself" dissolves. The significance of the imprisonment image applied to the human
spirit is evident in Yakov's continued reflection: "If

you're not lucky your thoughts can poison you." Yakov's glib condition, "if you're lucky," implies, of course, a much more profound condition, one which emerges as the developing character of Yakov emerges: the unaccountable-for possession of the will to be free to live a life. Yakov's will to live is presented as the strongest directing force in his character.

In a climactic scene in the episode depicting Yakov's achivement of freedom to celebrate the given world of his existence, Malamud presents contrasting images of Yakov's day in the cell, images first of a death-in-life existence, then images of living existence. Yakov's achievement of freedom to accept the limitations of the one and of the freedom to be open to the experience of the other marks the first major change in the presentation of his developing sensibility:

> During the day there were the regular checks through the spy hole, and three depressing searches of his body. There were cleaning out ashes, and making and lighting the stove. There was the sweeping of the cell to do, urinating in the can, walking back and forth until one began to count; or sitting at the table with nothing to do. There was the going for, and eating of, his meager meals. There was trying to remember and trying to forget. There was the counting of each day; there was reciting the psalm he had put together. He also watched the light and dark change. The morning dark had a little freshness, a little anticipation in it, though what he anticipated he could not say. The night dark was heavy with thickened and compounded shadows. In the morning the shadows unfurled until only one was left, that which lingered in the cell all day. It was gone for a minute near eleven he guessed, when a beam of sunlight, on days the sun appeared, touched the corroded inner wall a

foot above his mattress, a beam of golden light gone in a few minutes. Once he kissed it on the wall. Once he licked it with his tongue.

We see that now although still imprisoned, Yakov ironically is capable of a fuller and richer experience than he was capable of in the shtetl.

The immediate consequence of his new spiritual freedom is Yakov's reflection about his past life. In one instance he remembers the impact that reading Spinoza had on his developing character:

> I picked up books here and there, a few I stole, and read by the lamp. Many times after I read I slept on the kitchen bench. When I was reading Spinoza I stayed up night after night. I was by now excited by ideas and I tried to collect a few of my own. It was the beginning of a different Yakov.

The "different Yakov" image is a thematic one; it occurs in several points throughout the novel, each time symbolizing a new stage of freedom for Yakov. What is significant here is Yakov's new-found desire for awareness, his reflection on that point in his life when he became "excited by ideas." The "different Yakov" here, of course, is the Yakov who has transcended his physical and spiritual imprisonment to the degree that his life in prison, although still as miserable as ever, is no longer the central reality of his existence. Now what is most real is his freedom to live, however limited that living may be.

In the course of his free reflections, he comes presently to his relationship with his wife Raisl: "I scratch at memory. I think of Raisl." He recalls the beginning of his relationship with her and in the process reveals something of her early limitations and something of his early propensity "to make a free man of himself":

> One day in the woods we became man and wife. She
> said no but took a chance. Later it bothered her.
> She was afraid for her child once she had one, that
> it would be born crippled or with seven fingers.
> "Don't be superstitious," I said. "If you want to be
> free, first be free in your mind."

And in the continuing process of his reflection, he comes
to the experience of a new concept of freedom, one
which advances Malamud's increasingly complex theme:
Freedom of the spiritual self is a necessary condition
for freedom in a relationship with another.

> At first I cursed her like somebody in the Bible curses
> his whorish wife. "May she keep her miscarrying
> womb and dry breasts." But now I look at it like
> this: She had tied herself to the wrong future.

Again the changed Yakov! And we see that his response
is presented as the direct result of his degree of freedom
to make it. It is at this point that he can realize that
some of the guilt for the failure of the marriage is his:

> Yakov reveried the past; the shtetl, the mistakes and
> failures of his life. One white-mooned night, after a
> bitter quarrel about something he couldn't remember
> now, Raisl had left the hut and run in the dark to
> her father. The fixer, sitting alone, thinking over his
> bitterness and the falseness of his accusations, had
> thought of going after her but had gone to sleep in-
> stead. After all, he was dead tired doing nothing. The
> next year the accusation against her had come true,
> although it wasn't true then. Who had made it come
> true? If he had run after her then, would he be sitting
> here now?

It is now in his new capability to see his relationship
with his wife as something real apart from his own

hostilities and defensive feelings that Yakov can ask, "Who had made it [his accusation] come true?" His question reveals his realization that he has participated in his wife's unfaithfulness, that his unconcern was itself an act which she had responded to and that he also is guilty for it.

And the bitterness that he feels for Raisl is no longer present when she is permitted to visit the prison, ostensibly to further the plan of his persecutors by getting him to sign a false confession, but actually to plead with him to recognize her infant son who was not fathered by Yakov. The scene is touching and brilliantly executed. We see Yakov's gentleness, his objectivity, and his acceptance of his wife—an acceptance that did not possess the same particular quality in their earlier relationship. What is revealed, of course, is the Yakov Bok who has achieved what he had once intellectualized as the Spinoza aim: "to make a free man out of himself." At first he upbraids Raisl because he believes that she has come "to get me to confess lies I've resisted for two years. To betray me again." Raisl's answer, after assuring him that "It was the only way I could get in," echoes one of Malamud's most persistent themes: "But it's not why I came, I came to cry." And presently: " 'What are you crying for?' he asked. 'For you, for me, for the world.' "

Like Yakov, Raisl too has found meaning in her suffering, climaxed now by her being ostracized by the community. But the most significant change is in Yakov: "As she wept she moved him. He had learned about tears." When he speaks to Raisl, it is out of a self freed from bitterness: " 'I've thought about our life from beginning to end and I can't blame you for more than I blame myself.' " Yakov's decision is, of course, to acknowledge the child as his own. His comment reveals his humanity:

for whom he is an effective instrument. Together both Grubeshov and the establishment embody a political form which is devoid of any concern for the individual human being, but one finally which Yakov in his freedom is strong enough to resist.

Yakov's earlier response to the establishment, that which followed his arrest and interrogation, was a response of panic and fear. His response after two and one half years of suffering in prison is the complete opposite. Now in place of an imprisoning fear he experiences a freedom to respond. And now his response is hate. The change is evident when he is summoned by Grubeshov to the courthouse, ostensibly to be presented with his indictment:

> Grubeshov coughed seriously and glanced away. Yakov saw no papers on his desk. Though he had made up his mind to be controlled before this archanti-Semite, he could not help himself and began to shiver. He had been trembling within and had suppressed it, but when he thought of what had happened to Bibikov, and how he himself had been treated and what he had endured because of Grubeshov, a bone of hatred thickened in his throat and his body shook. It trembled violently as though it were trying to expel a poisonous substance. And though he was ashamed to be shivering as though feverish or freezing in front of this man, he could not stop it.

The suggestion is clear that Yakov's feeling of hate is objectively justified as a free response to the embodiment of evil that Grubeshov represents. But what is also suggested is the fundamental change in Yakov, a change engendered by his experience of new limits to his intellectual and existential responses as a fulfilled human being.

Some of those new limits become evident at once when the spiritually limited Yakov Bok of the period before his imprisonment is recalled. On the night before his trial, after two and a half years in prison, he is aware of a basic change in himself. We remember his anxieties and unfounded fears and his passive timidity before the drunken, Jew-hating, Black Hundred's Russian to whom he gave assistance. Now, after his long imprisonment, he can declare in a dream conversation with his spiritual advisor, Bibikov, who has been victimized by the Russians:

> "Your honor, I've had an extraordinary insight."
> "You don't say? What is it?"
> "Something in myself has changed. I'm not the same man I was. I fear less and hate more."

The climax of the novel occurs when Yakov is forced by nearly unbearable tortures to decide whether or not he should take his own life. He is chained to the wall in a freezing cell, unable to lie down unless released by the guard:

> After a while all he thought of was death. He was terribly weary, hungry to rid himself of the hard chains and the devilishly freezing cell. He hoped to die quickly, to end his suffering for once and all, to get rid of all he was and had been. His death would mean there was one last choice, there always is, and he had taken it.

At this point he decides to force the guards to kill him, by refusing to obey the order to undress for the sixth search of the day, his purpose to involve the establishment:

> They want me to die but not directly by their hand. They'll keep me in chains, making searches until my

heart gives out. Then they can say I died of natural causes "while awaiting trial." I'll make it unnatural causes. I'll make it by their hand. I'll provoke them to kill me.

Then in a dream in which he sees the kindly Shmuel, Raisl's father, lying in a coffin, he "awakens, grieving, his beard damp with salt tears." His response to the dream is immediate; it is a response that underlies his decision not to commit suicide: " 'Live Shmuel,' he sighs. 'Live. Let me die for you.' " It is at this point that Yakov realizes just how he can die for Shmuel, that is, for the whole Jewish community: by not taking his own life. He realizes that Shmuel and countless others may die if the Russians "work up a pogrom in celebration of his death." And then occurs his most significant act, a commitment of his life by his decision to live. It is a commitment directly related to his having "made a free man out of himself," which, in turn, is directly related to his suffering and his response to it:

what do I get by dying outside of release from pain? what have I earned if a single Jew dies because I did? Suffering I can gladly live without, I hate the taste of it, but if I must suffer let it be for something. Let it be for Shmuel.

Yakov's commitment is at once an expression of the theme of the novel: Freedom of the self allows man to "join the universe"; the universe to which Yakov refers is, of course, the universe of humanity. In the episode in which the guard Kogin draws his gun against the deputy warden in an unpremeditated response to save Yakov's life, there is a striking parallel with the central theme of the novel. Kogin in the depths of his own personal tragedy as an anguished father whose son has destroyed his own life is now able, because of his suffering, to see his prisoner as also a suffering human being.

Yakov is no longer simply the embodiment of a concept, i.e., a Jewish ritual murderer or a "Christ killer."
When Yakov is intentionally provoked beyond his own
endurance into a fit of rage—giving the deputy warden
the justification he has sought to kill him in order that
he would not be brought to a trial in which the establishment had no real evidence against him—Kogin inter-
feres:

> "Hold on a minute, your honor," said Kogin to the
> Deputy Warden. His deep voice broke. "I've listened
> to this man night after night, I know his sorrows.
> Enough is enough, and anyway it's time for his trial
> to begin."
> "Get out of my way or I'll cite you for insubordi-
> nation, you son-of-a-bitch." Kogin pressed the muzzle
> of his revolver against the Deputy Warden's neck.
> Berezhinsky reached for his gun but before he
> could draw, Kogin fired. He fired at the ceiling and
> after a while dust drifted to the floor.
> A whistle sounded shrilly in the corridor. The
> prison bell clanged. The iron cell door was slammed
> open and the white-faced captain and his Cossack
> guards rushed into the cell.
> "I've given my personal receipt," he roared.
> "My head aches," Kogin muttered. He sank to his
> knees with blood on his face. The Deputy Warden
> had shot him.

The point is that when Kogin transcends his role as an
instrument of the establishment he frees himself in a
new allegiance, one born out of the experienced recognition of another's suffering. Like Yakov, he "joins the
universe" of humanity. In attending to what is real
about Yakov's situation, Kogin responds now not out
of indoctrination but out of his new free self, out of his
new sense of shared humanity.

In the closing episode the image of Yakov being carried through the streets is in direct contrast to the same marching image which followed his arrest. Then he was presented as a man "in a state of unrelieved distress," one who "begged the colonel to let him walk on the sidewalk to lessen his embarrassment." Now with "the masses of people gathered on both sides of the street," Yakov is not only unashamed but composed and proud:

> "Yakov Bok!" he called out. "Yakov Bok!"
> The Cossack riding on the left side of the carriage, a thick-shouldered man with overhanging brows and a mustache turning gray, gazed impassively ahead; but the rider cantering along on the door side, a youth of twenty or so on a gray mare, from time to time stole a glance at Yakov when he was staring out the window, as though trying to measure his guilt or innocence.
> "Innocent!" the fixer cried out to him. "Innocent!"

His spiritual composure and inner freedom are reflected also in the old whimsical detachment which had been absent throughout his imprisonment: "And though he had no reason to, he smiled a little at the Cossack for his youth and good looks, and for being, as such things go, a free man, give or take a little." One somber image thrusts the reader back to the work's opening images, functioning to unite the presentations in that overall single presentation which is the work: "Amid the crowd were a few Jews watching with commiseration or fear."

It is interesting to note that in the final short section of the book, the resolution of the problem of Yakov Bok's external freedom is not offered; it is not the thematic problem of the novel.

Notes

1 – The Formalist Approach to the Criticism of Fiction

1. Immanuel Kant, *The Critique of Aesthetic Judgment*, trans. J. H. Bernard (London, 1931), p. 45.

2. Ibid., p. 63.

3. Theodore Meyer Greene, *The Arts and the Art of Criticism* (Princeton, N. J., 1940), p. 354.

4. John Crowe Ransom, "Criticism as Pure Speculation," in *The Intent of the Critic*, ed. D. A. Stauffer (Princeton, 1941), p. 113.

5. Ransom, *The World's Body* (New York, 1938), p. 111.

6. Greene, p. 242.

7. Ransom, *The World's Body*, p. 44.

8. Stephen Spender, "The Making of a Poem," *Partisan Review* 13 (Summer 1946), p. 301.

9. T. S. Eliot, *Selected Essays, 1917–1932* (London, 1932), p. 145.

10. Ezra Pound, "A Few Don'ts by an Imagiste," *Poetry* 1 (1912), p. 200.

11. Aldous Huxley, "The Education of an Amphibian," *Adonis and the Alphabet* (London, 1956), pp. 14–15.

2 – Joyce's "The Dead"

1. Bernard Benstock, *Joyce–Again's Wake* (Seattle, 1965), pp. 3–4.

2. Wayne C. Booth, *The Rhetoric of Fiction* (Chicago, 1961), p. 325.

3. Ibid.

4. Greene, *The Arts*, p. 12.

5. Booth, p. 325.

6. Kant, *Aesthetic Judgment*, p. 208.

7. Booth, p. 329–31.

8. Ibid., p. 335.

Index